Law And The Administration Of Justice In The Twenty-First Century

Edited By

Hon. Justice I. A. Umezulike

First Published 1997 by
FOURTH DIMENSION PUBLISHING CO., LTD
16 Fifth Avenue, City Layout. PMB. 01164, Enugu, Nigeria.
Tel+234-42-459969. Fax+234-42-456904.
email: fdpbooks@aol.com, fdpbooks@yahoo.com
Web site: http://www.fdpbooks.com.

Reprinted 2002

ISBN 978-156-425-3

Photoset and printed in Nigeria by
Fourth Dimension Publishers, Enugu.

Table Of Contents

Dedication

This work is dedicated to all persons of the world who believe and know that *Jesus Christ* is *God Almighty.*

Acknowledgement

We acknowledge with great debt of gratitude, the prompt response of all those who presented papers at the July 17th 1997 Workshop, at a very short notice. The luminous papers form the essential bulk of this publication. Our special thanks are due to Professors S.M.C. Obi and C.O. Okonkwo for their prompt response despite the short notice. This is evidence of their unremitting fidelity to legal education and development.

Our gratitude also goes to the Enugu Branch of the Nigerian Bar Association organised under the dynamic and refreshingly committed leadership of Dr. A.O. Mogbo S.A.N. for its invaluable assistance in hosting the One-day Workshop.

Finally, profound gratitude is owed OUR LORD AND SAVIOUR JESUS CHRIST for the enabling climate from which our little idea fructified to reality. To HIM (Jesus Christ) are all thanks and praises due.

Hon. Justice I. A. Umezulike
(Editor)

Preface

On the 17th day of July 1997 a one-day workshop under the theme "*Law and the Administration of Justice In the Twenty-first Century*" was held at the Enugu Law Development Centre in honour of the retiring Chief Judge of Enugu State, Hon. Justice Eze Ozobu. The contrivance was entirely mire.

This book therefore contains some of the papers presented at the Workshop. However because of space-constraints we are unable to include all the presented papers. For the same reason, the other papers were rigorously edited to come within the pagination limit dictated by our reputable publishers.

The book contains six chapters. Each chapter holds a peculiar strength. However, because the taste of the pudding is entirely in the eating, one is discharged from presenting any prefatory remarks on the chapters, that may prevent the reader from going to the source. But I seek leave to commend Chapter Two of this book to the intimate reading of all judges in Nigeria especially the Justices of the Supreme Court. It is hoped that the critical reading of the said Chapter may result in the modification or rectification of the general judicial stand taken by the apex court in *Alhaji Abubakar Sadiku* v. *Alhaji Abba Dalori (1996) 4 N.W.L.R.* (pt. 400) p. 769, that the High Courts have no jurisdiction in land matters originating from non-urban area of a state.

Chapter Three also holds special appeal to judges and practitioners currently faced with legal headaches in Failed Bank Tribunals.

The remainder, I confidently commend to all, in the legal profession who are interested in current legal developments. The design is to present an *important tool* for researchers, professors, legal practitioners, judges and intelligent men of all classes rather than *another supply of material*. We apologise to our colleagues and presenters whose papers could not be included herein. We shall give the papers priority when the next opportunity presents itself.

The law and issues discussed in this book are as they stand on or before the 17th day of July, 1997.

Hon. Justice I.A. Umezulike
(Editor)

CHAPTER 1

Debriefing Counsel In Trial Proceedings Overview And Some Observations

By
Justice I.A. Umezulike
High Court Enugu

Introduction

This presentation is prompted by the terse but far reaching decision of the Supreme Court in *Chief M.K.O. Abiola v. Federal Republic of Nigeria*[1]. In the terse decision Belgore J.S.C. who read the leading ruling of the Supreme Court, said:

> the big issue is who is representing the appellant. One counsel filed motion to withdraw a subsisting appeal and Chief Ajayi's objection as to competency of this panel hearing it is now to be decided: The best person to decide who represents him as counsel is the appellant and that is his constitutional right. To my mind, the energy of the parties should be directed to the appellant to intimate his choice. Time honoured practice is for this issue of representation to be decided by counsel after consulting the appellant or the appellant writing to intimate his choice of counsel or by any other means, e.g. affidavit showing who will be his counsel. It is always a privilege, *the matter* of counsel-client relationship and I do not believe it is right to involve the court in this.[2]

If I understood the above observation correctly, it does seem to me to remove the question of representation of counsel from the purview of the court. It locates the question firmly in the litigant/party over whom the legal practitioners are contesting for representation. Again if I understood the above reasoning correctly it means that where two counsel are in contest over who represents a party in a court, the court is not entitled to pronounce on which counsel upon the facts presented before him, is entitled to represent the party. The court must adjourn the case and advise the contesting counsel to have access to the litigant or party to give his instructions in writing,[3] or by his swearing to an affidavit,[4] or even writing a letter under his own long hand[5] or by his swearing to an affidavit[6] or even writing a letter under his own longhand to the trial[7] court and the contending counsel.[8]

Coming from the apex court of the land the above observation is characterised with finality not only for the parties involved but for the lower courts of the land. But its finality on those spheres, does not foreclose any academic commentary that could be made upon the decision.

The above decision presupposes that the party involved is a physical person who can always be reached for his letter, affidavit or physical presence to decide the matter. It does not accommodate juristic persons such as companies, universities and other institutions where authorities to act are diffused and there is a kind of devolution of authority into so many heads. For example, assuming two counsel are contesting over who should represent the University of Lagos in a matter in court, the Pro-Chancellor writes to court to say, the university recognises Mr. A., while the Vice-Chancellor writes to say, the university recognises Mr. B. and the Registrar writes to say, the university recognises Mr. C. what would the court do in the circumstance? From the principle set forth above by the Supreme Court, it seems the court would do nothing but toss the matter back to these various authorities in the university and hope for the best. The same situation would present itself if the matter relates to a company and there are conflicting letters from the Chairman and the Managing Director; or in a ministry and the conflicting letters issued from the Commissioner and the Director General. The examples would be multiplied further. Again, assuming a human being is involved but as in the case of Abiola is incarceration and incommunicado. Is the court before whom two lawyers have come to blows over representation not entitled to decide one way or another on the question based on the facts presented? Is it not practical, speedier and tidier that it does so having due regard to the facts before it? It is submitted that an affirmative answer is imperative. We shall however return to that anon.

However, the aim of this paper is to show how a counsel who has began a case on behalf of a party in court should be debriefed. We shall venture a few general comments.

1. How Is Counsel Briefed

We cannot really be talking of debriefing counsel, without knowing how he was briefed in the first place. There are three common modes of briefing. The first is oral and the other is written briefing. In very many cases especially where individuals or communities are involved, oral briefing of counsel is common. Sometimes it is done by telephone call. Where in the counsel is given the appropriate instruction to take up a matter.

The second mode of briefing is written. This is common among certain elite group, companies, corporations and institutions who have retainer-counsel. The written document in this regard spells out the tenure of the retainership and the type of cases to be handled by the counsel. A specific letter authorising appearance of counsel for an institution or company in a particular case may still be necessary where there are many counsel in the retainership of the company or institution.

The third mode of briefing is where the court under the law provides counsel for an accused person. This third mode is uncommon and in any case does not provide any problem.

Evidently the mode of briefing of counsel is relevant in deciding whether or not he has been effectually and properly debriefed. That is not however to say that counsel who was briefed orally by an individual litigant or accused cannot be removed by a written letter or vise-versa. But where institutions and companies are involved documentary briefing and debriefing make the matter less contentious. But even at that level problems do arise. For instance if in a university say, the Pro-Chancellor could does a letter retaining `A' for a case and the Vice-Chancellor briefs `B' or does another letter for B in respect of the same case; or in a company, the Chairman does a letter retaining A and the Managing Director or General Manager as the case may be, does another for `B' in respect of the same case.

It is submitted that the authority to retain counsel must be located where the control to the day to day running of the company, institution or establishment lay. It is therefore to be surmised that the authority to retain a counsel must lie with the official who is incharge of the day to day running of the outfit or company.

Thus upon the examination of the law or statute establishing the institution or company, the right to retain must therefore be said to rest in the officer to whom the statute or law rests the day to day running of the outfit. So if it is the Pro Chancellor or Vice Chancellor or Registrar in the case of a university, then the power to brief and debrief must rest in him. In the case of a company, if the Chairman or Managing Director or the General Manager, is the person incharge of the day to day running of the company, then in him must the power to brief or debrief lie.

In *Professor Emea Arua v. University of Nigeria and another*[9] the Nsukka High Court felt its way through the intricate web of facts presented in the case. The plaintiff, a professor of Agric-Economic had commenced action against the University and its registrar for declarative and injunctive reliefs. The university's retainer counsel commenced the defence of the defendants, namely the university and its registrar at the written instance of the Vice Chancellor. In the course of the proceedings, the Pro Chancellor of the University who was the Chairman of counsel wrote two letters. One of the letters appointed another counsel to take over the case from the University's retainer-counsel. The second letter from the Pro-Chancellor was one purportedly debriefing the University's retainer-counsel who was handling the case. Thus the court was faced with two vital but conflicting letters from two paramount officers of the institution.

Of note, however, is that at the time the Pro Chancellor wrote the said letters, which for purposes of this presentation, we may refer to as exhibits A and B; the University Council which he was its Chairman was under the hammer of the court's interim injunction, which, for better or for worse, rightly or wrongly at the time, remanded its convocation and functioning pending the determination of the matter before the court. So when the Pro-Chancellor wrote exhibits `A' and `B' did he do so dehors the council or as chairman of council whose functioning had been stirelised or castrated by an injunctive order of the court. It was urged upon the court by the Senior Counsel who was appointed by the said *exhibit `A'* above that the Pro-Chancellor could do those letter on behalf of Council not withstanding that the Council was in limbo under what he called the doctrine of necessity. The response of the court to this legal headache is noteworthy. It said:

> the doctrine of civil necessity is of municipal application. It does not apply and should not be extended to the domestic fora of artificial legal entities such as the university whose powers are limited by the doctrine of ultra-veres to what is authorised by the University of Nigeria Act. cap. 459 Laws of the Federation 1990. Consequently if the doctrine of civil necessity does not apply to the University, it shall therefore not avail its Pro-Chancellor to do *exhibit `A'*.[10]

On the question as to who has the power to brief and debrief counsel in the circumstances presented in that university system, the court examined sections 4,5, and 7 of the University of Nigeria Act Cap 459 and came to the following conclusions:

> the functions of the governing council of the first defendant which are enrobed in section 5 of Cap 459 were deliberately made applicable to the entire body of the governing council of the first defendant. It is clearly wrong to think of the Pro-Chancellor and the Chairman of Council as the repository of the powers and functions of the Council. I have also taken the firm view in this ruling that the doctrine of civil necessity ably expoused by the second Senior Counsel does not avail the Pro Chancellor in the instant case. If it did it would vitiate the entire Act i.e. Cap 459 and reduce the entire university to Sole-Administratorship. But unfortunately Cap 459 is still extant. Its delimitation of powers and allocation of functions between its principal organs are self evident. Consequently in the absence of proper

convocation of the Governing Council of the first defendant to give approval to *exhibit 1A'* it remains ineffective and meaningless.[11]

The court therefore proceeded to reject exhibits `A' and `B' which were letters from the Pro-Chancellor purportedly debriefing the University's retainer-counsel and appointing another counsel for the university. It held that under the university system it was the duty of the Vice Chancellor to brief or debrief counsel for the institution. In coming to this conclusion the court said:

> in the day to day running of the University including its administrative, academic and support systems, the Vice Chancellor to the exclusion of any other person or authority including the Pro-Chancellor is incharge or the Chief Executive. In fact sections 15, 16,17 and 22 of Cap 459 reinforce the status of the Vice Chancellor as the Chief Executive of the University and demonstrate that the power of control and management of the first defendant i.e. the University or its day to day running is not bifurcated. It lies with the Vice-Chancellor. The point which I strive to make is that in the present circumstances of the first defendant and having regard to the provisions of Cap 459, it would be irregular, and illegal to engage or disengage a counsel for the university or contract same to take on a major case for the university without the approval, direction and consent of its chief executive, the Vice-Chancellor.[12]

It therefore seems to us undoubted that in institutions, organisations and companies, the power to engage, disengage or brief and debrief counsel must rest with the Chief Executive who is incharge of the day to day running of the institution, organisation or company. But when he does exercise this power, he must inform all the principal officers of the organisation including any nominal head of the place.

Responsibility Upon Being Briefed

The responsibility of counsel upon being briefed is set out under the rules of court and settled upon superior authorities.

Under Order 34 Rules 1 and 2 it is enacted as follows:

> (1) Every legal practitioner engaged to conduct a case before the court shall be deemed to be an officer of the court for purposes of such case
>
> (2) Every legal practitioner who shall be engaged in any course or matter shall be bound to conduct the same on behalf of the party for whom he shall have been so engaged until final judgement, unless allowed by the court for any special reason to cease from acting therein; but he shall not be bound, except under express agreement or unless re-engaged, to take any proceedings in relation to any proceedings after the judgement.

It is clear from the above that once a counsel has been duly briefed to handle a case, he becomes not only an officer of the court intent on doing his best for his client but must prosecute the case till final judgement unless with leave of court, he withdraws from the case.

In *Professor J.C. Edozien v. Chief O. Edozien*[13] the Supreme Court, per Karibi-Whyte J.S.C. said:

> ordinarily a counsel is retained by a client to conduct a cause without any limitation. The apparent authority with which he is clothed when he appears to conduct the cause is to do everything which in the exercise of his discretion may be the best for the interest of his client in the conduct of the cause.[14]

Seven year earlier, the Supreme Court, this time per Esho J.S.C. had this to say:

> a lawyer is a professional visa-vis a client he is on contract and his professional skill hired by the client is to be employed at his discretion. After all he is employed to deal with learned men in learned surroundings and he himself is learned, which the client even if he is a lawyer himself, is not learned for the purposes of the case.[15]

It is also scarcely arguable that the relationship of client-counsel is contractual. It is regulated by the general principles of law of contract. There must be definite offer by client and definite acceptance by counsel. If there is no definite offer by the client any foray into the clients's case by counsel would amount to touting and unprofessional conduct. In communities, families and town unions say, such offer must proceed from the head or at least receive his approval or consent.

How To Debrief Counsel

Usually when a client is not satisfied with the handling of his case by counsel or for other meta-legal reasons does not want the counsel to continue to prosecute his case, the most honourable method of disengaging him is to write to him privately, follow it up with a visit to the counsel's chambers to pay all outstanding fees due to him and collect his case-file for transfer to any new counsel he may wish to engage. Thus debriefing implies the termination of the services of counsel in a particular case. The client is free to debrief counsel at any time in the proceedings for good reasons or for no reasons at all provided he had perfected the brief of the counsel sought to be debriefed. Whilst counsel requires special reason to withdraw from a case, his client seems to me as free as air to debrief him in the circumstances heretofore stated.

Where counsel is recalcitrant in handing over the case file to the client, the client can come to court to publicly announce his debriefing of the counsel. The court should however never allow such a public disgrace of counsel unless it became absolutely inevitable. The court must strain every nerve to prevent it. In *F.R.N. v. Abiola,16* the Court of Appeal, per Kalgo J.C.A. prickly but rightly asked the question:

> what power has the trial court to order the respondent to come and pick a counsel of his own choice in open court.

However problems do arise when two counsel have come to blows over who should represent a client in a case. The scenario is no longer infrequent. With scarcely a pause for breath one can tick off the many instances such situation had confronted one on one's fairly young experience on the bench. It constitutes a great disgrace to the highly venerated legal profession and practice in Nigeria. What is to be done? We think that the starting point is to say that an appointer of counsel is the only person entitled to debrief him.Until he does so to the clear notice of the court in which the case pends, any other counsel who makes an appearance under whatsoever guise for the same client must either be ignored, strongly reprimanded and treated as a tout. It must be noted that counsel when ever he takes up a case in court has become an officer of court for purposes of that case.[17] Such an officer of court shall not be shoved off the court by a stranger to his original contract with his client, namely, the new counsel writing to take over the case. However counsel who has been briefed to take over a case from another counsel must first of all ascertain:

(1) Whether the client has communicated his appointment to the counsel from whom he is contracted to take over.
(2) Whether the client had paid all outstanding fees to the counsel.
(3) Whether the client had duly notified the court.
(4) Whether the former counsel had withdrawn his appearance in the case.

If all the above conditions are not satisfied, it would be wicked, unprofessional, lack of professional fidelity and shameful for another counsel to enter appearance and seek to take over from the former counsel.

In this regard, it is vain and unacceptable to seek to overthrow your colleague or effect the change by way of motion on notice as is the case in some states of Nigerian Federation. It is also unsalusbrious for the new counsel to write the other counsel asking him (the other counsel) to stay away from the case because he has been briefed in the case.

In *F.R.N. v. Abiola18,* a senior counsel wrote to another senior counsel handling Abiola's case thus:

> Dear Sir,
>
> You are hereby notified that Chief Afe Babalola S.A.N. and I have been duly instructed to assume the conduct of the defence of Bashorun M.K.O. Abiola in the prosecution against him, as well as ancillary or incidental proceedings arising therefrom or connected therewith. Please let me know if you wish to contest our authority to represent the Bashorun. In that event, you will be notified of any proceedings we may take on behalf of the Bashorun and we shall arrange for him to be produced in court so that the question of the counsel of his choice can be settled summarily by direct inquiry from him in open court.

The above note is an invitation to a skirmish. And it is clearly a spit in the face of a colleague at the bar who had committed no offence in taking up his client's case. Is counsel's public disgrace in open court the better way to debrief him? Why did the two learned Senior Counsel wishing to take over the case not wait until all the above listed conditions were satisfied before making their eminent appearance in the case. Not withstanding the lucre and material benefits which a case holds or promises, the amity and solidarity in the legal profession need not be sacrificed or endangered.

However where the client over whose representation two lawyers are at war, is incarcerated or in custody of the state, the Supreme Court had suggested three methods of resolving the matter. In Abiola's case,[19] Belgore J.S.C. said:

> this could be in the form of any of three ways mentioned above, namely by having physical access to him to give his instructions in writing, or by his swearing to an affidavit, or even writing a letter under his long hand to the trial court and the contending counsel[20]

Until the client adopts' any of the above methods, must the court go on vacation over the matter? It is submitted that until the client takes any of the above steps to effectually debrief his former counsel, the case must go on with him. The court must rule the new counsel out of the proceedings. Courts should not run away from taking decisions. The court's insistence upon counsel concluding a case he had taken up for his client does not seem to be an abstraction or infraction upon the constitutional right of counsel, until the appointor of the counsel evinces a contrary intention. After all the counsel's duty under the rules is to prosecute the case up to judgement stage. It is certainly not a matter which the court would throw back to the disputants to resolve amongst themselves and rise happily for the day. Our court should lay down the principles and set the standards. As we have hinted earlier, only an appointor can debrief. Thus if `A' has briefed counsel for a case, A's son or wife or brother cannot debrief him. Similarly if a head of community, family or organisation has briefed counsel, a principal member no matter how powerful he is cannot debrief the counsel. The examples could be further multiplied. Suffice it to say that it is not proper for or competent of a legal practitioner no matter the attractions in the case, to amble into a court to announce that a counsel previously handling a case had been debriefed and that he was taking over the prosecution of the case. This approach is despicable, dishonourable and approximating touting.

It may well be that to avoid this constant disgraceful skirmishes in our court, it is now desired that counsel filing an action for a party in court must do so with the party's written authorisation to handle the case. And in the event of conflict between two counsel in respect of representation, the court shall look solely to the court's file to see whether, the earlier written authorisation had been counter-manded or cancelled by a subsequent letter from the party or client. If the answer is in the affirmative, then the new counsel would be let into the case, but if the answer is in the negative, then the new counsel must be ruled out the proceedings.

General Comment/Conclusion

The ubiquity of this problem may bear upon the practitioners to insist upon pre-trial full payment of their professional fees. And because of the harsh economic situation in the country, this may affect the case-flow in our courts because only few litigants would be in a position to meet the situation of pretrial full payment of counsel's professional fees. The legal profession and practice in Nigeria are regulated by laws, rules, regulations and decorous conventions. Members of the profession who are expected to be repository of due process should never expose themselves to situations where touting could be named after them. A lawyer should not be placed in a position where he has to be accepting a brief with the detective's eye, anticipating dishonesty, summary debriefing from his client and lawlessness or anomie from his colleagues at the Bar.

Fighting and disputation over representation of a client by two counsel in court is a conduct driven out of the legal profession more than a century ago in Britain and other civilised countries of the world. But this unhealthy exile has been welcomed into Nigeria by even the senior members of the legal profession.

Of course, if the trend is not reversed or the tendency extirpated, the legal profession would merely stagger into the 21st Century and break down utterly.

Notes

(1) (1997) 2 N.W.L.R. pt. 488 p.439
(2) *Ibid*, at 442
(3) *Ibid* at 443
(4) Ibidem
(5) Ibidem
(6) Ibidem
(7) IbidemN.W.L.R.(pt.32) p.767
(8) Ibidem
(9) Unreported Suit No. N/231/94 of 10/3/95
(10) Ibidem
(11) Ibidem
(12) Ibidem
(13) (1993) 1 N.W.L.R. (pt. 272) p. 678
(14) Ibid at p. 703
(15) Festus Adewunmi v.Plastex Nigeria Ltd (1986) 3
(16) (1997) 2 N.W.L.R. pt. 488 p.444
(17) See Order 34 Rule 1.

CHAPTER 2

Ouster Of High Courts' Jurisdiction: State High Courts And Customary Rights Of Occupancy

By
Prof. S.N.C. Obi
(Dean, Faculty of Law, Nnamdi Azikiwe University, Awka)

On Tuesday, April 23, 1996, our Supreme Court "telled the knell of parting" State High Courts in Nigeria. That was in the unfortunate case of *Alhaji Abubakar Sadikwu V. Alhaji Abba Dalori,* Where the Supreme Court said with one voice that a State High Court lacks original jurisdiction in case in which title to or rights in customary rights of Occupancy are in issue.

Customary rights of occupancy granted or deemed to have been granted by local governments constitute the vast majority of land holdings in this country. Most of the land disputes that come up for determination in the State High Courts (even in the metropolitan areas) are concerned with customary rights of occupancy. The Nigerian Bar, inner and outer alike, have a duty therefore to take a close look at this latest "Out of bounds" poster stuck up in the face of the State High Courts of this country.

The facts that are material to the Supreme Court Decision in the instant case are as follows. The land in dispute was allocated to the appellant, Alhaji Abubakar Sadikwu in January 1978 and to the respondent Alhaji Abba Dalori in June 1979 by the Maiduguri Local Authority/Maiduguri Metropolitan Council. Each of the allottees received his own separate Certificate of Customary Right of Occupancy issued by the Authority/Council.

There was no evidence that either of the two Certificates was ever converted into a statutory right of occupancy, nor was there any evidence that the locus in quo was ever declared an Urban area.

The simple claim before the Borno High Court in the suit was a declaration that the plaintiff (appellant in the Supreme Court) was the lawful owner of the land in dispute measuring 100ft by 300ft situate along Baga Road, Maiduguri, damages and an injunction. There were five defendants.

The trial High Court (Kolo J, as he then was) on the evidence before him entered judgment for the plaintiff as claimed. Dis-satisfied, the defendant appealed to the Court of Appeal sitting in Jos. There he raised the issue whether the trial High Court had jurisdiction to entertain the suit, in that the land in dispute was the subject of a customary right of occupancy. The Court of Appeal unanimously held that the trial High Court lacked jurisdiction to entertain the plaintiff's claim in the first place.

Dissatisfied, the plaintiff appealed to the Supreme Court against the decision of the Court of Appeal. The first defendant alone contested the appeal.

The plaintiff in the trial High Court and the 1st defendant in that court shall hereafter in this discussion be referred to as the appellant and the respondent respectively, **The Sole Issue** before the Supreme Court was:

> whether the learned justices of the court of Appeal were correct in holding that the trial High Court lacked jurisdiction to entertain the plaintiff's claim

At the hearing of the appeal in the Supreme Court, "the parties did not show up in court;" nor did their counsel. However, the appeal was deemed as properly argued by virtue of Order 6 Rule 8 (6) of the Supreme Rules 1985, the Court being satisfied that hearing notices were served and that briefs of arguments were filed and exchanged.

The Supreme Court Judgment

The learned Justice of the Supreme Court, Wali, who delivered the lead judgment drew attention to the failure of the trial High Court to consider or rule upon the submission made before it by one of the defence counsel namely, that the Court lacked jurisdiction to entertain the plaintiff's suit. He then went on:-

> it was the contention of learned counsel for the appellant in his brief that the Court of Appeal was wrong in law in holding that the trial High Court had

no jurisdiction to entertain the appellant's case by virtue of S.41 of the Land Use Act, 1978 when by the time the appellant's case was filed in the High Court, the 1979 Constitution had not become operative and as such, the relevant laws applicable at the time were:-

(i) High Court Law (cap 59) Laws of Northern Nigeria, 1963 (Applicable to Borno State)

(ii) Land Tenure Law (cap 49) Laws of Northern Nigeria, 1963 (applicable to Borno State)

(iii) Land Use Act, 1978.

It was the submission of learned counsel for the appellant that since S.41 of the Land Use Act, 1978 prevails over S.41(2) of the Land Tenure Law, 1963 by virtue of the former being an Act deemed to have been enacted by the National Assembly while the latter is an existing Law deemed to have been enacted by the Borno State House of Assembly, therefore, the only provisions of the laws relevant for consideration to resolve the issue raised in this appeal are S.17(1) of the High Court Law of Northern Nigeria and S.41 of the Land Use Act read in conjunction with S.39 of the same Act. Learned counsel argued that S.17(1) of the High Court Law is subject to the provisions of both sections 39 and 41 of the Land Use Act, and that unlike S.39(1) of the Act which vests exclusive original jurisdiction in the High Court in proceedings in land which is subject of a Statutory Right of Occupancy granted by the Governor or deemed granted, the provision of S.41 of the Act which confers jurisdiction on Area Courts, Customary or other courts of equivalent jurisdiction in respect of proceedings involving land subject of a customary right of occupancy granted by a local government, does not make the jurisdiction conferred on those courts exclusive to them. He said this is so because the phrase "exclusive original jurisdiction" is omitted in S.41 of the Act unlike in S.39(1) of the same Act where it has been expressly stated. He concluded that the combined effect of S.39(1) and S.41 of the Land Use Act is that the High Court as well as the Area Courts and Customary Courts have concurrent original jurisdiction in respect of a land matter that involves a customary right of occupancy by a Local Government. Learned counsel referred to and relied on the following cases to further support his arguments: *Soye v. A.G. Federation (1986) 2 NWLR (Pt 24) 560 at 572-73, Jamal v. A.C.B. (1977) 11S.C. 77 and Inland Revenue v. Rezcallah (1962) All NLR 1 at 7.*

"He urged this Court to allow the appeal, set aside the decision of the Court of Appeal and restore the judgment of the trial court": 1996 NWLR (Part 447) 158-9.

On the submission of the learned counsel for the respondent, also as contained in his brief of argument, the lead judgment commented as follows:

"In reply to the submissions above, learned counsel for the respondent contended that S.41 of the Land Use Act, contrary to the appellant's submission, did not expand the jurisdiction of the High Court to cover matters in land subject to customary right of occupancy, and that the omission of the phrase "exclusive original jurisdiction" in that section, unlike in S.39(1) (a) of the *same* Act, is deliberate in order to preserve the jurisdiction of Grades I, II and III Areas Courts on the one hand and Upper Area Courts on the other hand. Learned counsel also submitted that jurisdiction or power of a court must be expressly provided as it is not a matter of inference. He cited *Ariyo v. Ogele* (1968) 1 All NLR 1 at p.8 in support, and then went on to say that both sections 39 and 41 of the Land Use Act, 1978 were considered by the Supreme Court in the case of *Bakin Salati v. Shehu* (1986) 1 S.C. 332; (1986) NWLR (Pt 15) 198 wherein it concluded that there is no ambiguity in the two sections as regards the original jurisdiction of the High Courts under S. 39 of the Act viz-a-viz that of the Area Courts/Customary Courts under S. 41 of the same Act.

Learned counsel therefore urged the Court to hold that S. 17(1) (a) of the High Court Law does not inhibit the jurisdiction conferred on that court by S. 39 (1) (a) of the Land Use Act but that *as a matter of practice and procedure in that court, it ousts the exercise of the original jurisdiction by it in respect of land subject to the jurisdiction of the Area/Customary Courts.* He urged the court to dismiss the appeal for want of merit": 1996 NWLR (Part 447) 159-160. (Emphasis supplied) The lead judgment next reviewed the facts of the case as presented in the trial High Court. It then set out and reviewed the statutory provisions that were said to govern the case as follows:

> with this background, I shall now proceed to examine the provisions of the laws referred to by counsel for the appellant in support of his contention that the High Court had jurisdiction to adjudicate in the matter.

Section 39 (1) and (2) of the Land Use Act, 1978 reads as follows:

> 39 (1): The High Court shall have exclusive original jurisdiction in respect of the following proceedings-
>
> (a) Proceedings in respect of any land subject of a statutory right of occupancy granted by the Military Governor or deemed to be granted by him under this Decree, and for the purpose of this paragraph 'proceedings' includes proceedings for a declaration of title to a statutory right of occupancy.

There is no ambiguity in this section that it confers exclusive original jurisdiction on the High Court in all proceedings concerning land the subject of a statutory right of occupancy:

> Granted or deemed to be granted by the Governor, and proceedings for a declaration for a title to a statutory right of occupancy involving such land Section 41 (1) of the Land Tenure Law (Cap. 59) Laws of Northern Nigeria 1963 and applicable to Borno State provides thus:
>
> (1) The High Court shall have exclusive original jurisdiction in the following proceedings:
>
> (a) Proceedings in which the right of the Governor or the Minister to grant a statutory right over any land is in dispute;

The provisions of both S.39 of the Land Use Act 1978 and S. 41 (1) of the Land Tenure Laws give exclusive original jurisdiction to the High Court in all matters affecting land subject to a grant of a statutory right of occupancy by the Governor. There is not any ambiguity or conflict either in or between the two sections of the Act and the Law.

On land subject to customary right of occupancy, section 41 of the Land Use Act provides as follows:-

> 41 An area court or customary court or other court of equivalent jurisdiction in a state shall have jurisdiction in respect of proceedings in respect of customary right of occupancy granted by a Local Government under this Decree; and for the purposes of this paragraph 'proceedings' includes proceedings for a declaration of title to a Customary Right of Occupancy...

While S.2 and subsection (a) of S.41 of the Land Tenure Law provide thus:

> 2 An area court of competent jurisdiction shall have jurisdiction in the following proceedings:

(a) Proceedings in respect of any land the subject of a statutory right of occupancy granted by a local authority or of a customary right of occupancy where all the parties are subject to the jurisdiction of area courts: subject nevertheless to the provisions of paragraph (b) of S.3.

"The provisions of S. 3 (b) referred to in S.2 (a) supra confer jurisdiction in the High Court and or in a Distinct Court, the latter within the limits prescribed in the District Court Law, to exercise jurisdiction in proceedings affecting land in similar situations as stated in S.2 (a) where one or more of the parties are not subject to the jurisdiction of Area Court or where there is no Native or Area Court of competent jurisdiction to entertain the proceedings.

"In substance the purpose of S.41 of the Land Use Act, 1978 and S.41 (2) (a) of the Land Tenure Law is the same. The provisions of the two laws provide for conferment of jurisdiction on Area or Customary Courts in respect of proceedings involving the statutory or customary right of occupancy granted by a Local Government or Local Authority. In my view S. 17 (1) of the High Court Law of Northern Nigeria applicable to Borno State goes to support S. 41 of the Land Use Act, 1978 and S. 41 (2) (a) of the Land Tenure Law. I cannot therefore see how S. 17 (1) of the High Court Law, by reading it with the provisions of sections 39 and 41 of the Land Use Act 1978 and S. 41 of the Land Tenure Law, can confer jurisdiction in land matters specifically excluded by those laws...

"The Land Tenure Law S. 41 (2) and the Land Use Act, 1978 Section 41 are all existing laws by virtue of S.274 (4) (b) of the 1979 Constitution as stated by the Court of Appeal, but I am afraid I disagree with the court below when it stated that 'at the time the suit was instituted on 19 the July, 1979 in the High Court the applicable law would be the relevant provisions of the Land Use Act since it was deemed to have been an Act of National Assembly, consequently S 41 prevailed over Section 41 (2) (a) of the Land Tenure Law (supra). Since both laws are existing laws by virtue of S.274 (4) (b), S. 41 of the Land Use Act shall only prevail over S. 41(1) and 2 (a) to the extent the latter is in conflict with the former. See *Salati v. Shehu* (1986) All NLR53 (1986) 1NWLR (Pl 15) 198 at 211 particularly at 61 where Uwais J.S.C. (as he then was) admirably and thoroughly dealt with an issue of a similar nature as in this case which involved the interpretation of sections 39 and 41 of the Land Use Act and S.41(1) and 2(a) of the Land Tenure Law relating to proceedings in respect of land subject to a statutory or customary right of occupancy granted either by the Governor or the Local Government, as the case may be. "The appeal lacks merit and it is dismissed. The order of the Court of Appeal declaring the proceedings in the High Court null and void is hereby affirmed."

comments

According to counsel for the appellant, three statutory provisions are relevant in determining the issue before the Supreme Court in this suit. These are the High Court Law of Northern Nigeria 1963 applicable in Bornor State, the Land Tenure Law and the Land Use Act. Let us take a look at the relevant provisions of these statutes. The **High Court** Law S. 17 (1) (a) reads as follows

> *subject to the provisions* of the Land Tenure Law and of *any other written law* the High Court shall not exercise original jurisdiction in any suit or matter which -
>
> (a) "raises any issue as to the title to land or as to the title to any interest in land *which is subject to the jurisdiction of a native court*" (Emphasis supplied). *The Land Tenure Law* in its S.41 stipulates, inter alia, circumstances in which the High Court and the Customary Courts respectively have jurisdiction in proceedings involving Customary rights of occupancy.
>
> 41. (1) The High Court shall have exclusive original jurisdiction in the following proceedings-
>
> (a) proceedings in which the right of the Governor or the Minister to grant a statutory right of occupancy over any land is in dispute;
>
> (2) A native court of competent jurisdiction shall have jurisdiction in the following proceedings-
>
> (a) proceedings in respect of any land the subject of a statutory right of occupancy granted by a native authority or of a customary right of occupancy *where all parties are subject to the jurisdiction of native courts*, subject nevertheless to the provisions of paragraph (b) of subsection (3):
>
> (3) The High Court and District Court (within the respective limits prescribed in the District Courts Law) shall have jurisdiction in the following proceedings-

(a) proceedings in respect of any land the subject of a statutory right of occupancy granted by a native authority or of a customary right of occupancy *where one or more of the parties are not subject to the jurisdiction of native courts;*

(b) proceedings of the description referred to in paragraph (a) of subsection (2) *where there is no native court of competent jurisdiction available to try the proceedings;*

(c) proceedings in respect of any land the subject of any right of occupancy other than those otherwise specifically described in this section.

(4) "proceedings in respect of any land the subject of a right of Occupancy" shall include proceedings for a declaration of title to a right of occupancy.

The Land Use Act, in S. 39 and S. 41, provides for jurisdiction for the High Court and for Customary Courts (or their equivalents) in matters relating to rights of occupancy as follows:-

39. (1) The High Court shall have exclusive original jurisdiction in respect of the following proceedings:

(a) proceedings in respect of any land the subject of a statutory right of occupancy granted by the Governor or deemed to be granted by him under this Act, and for the purposes of this paragraph 'proceedings' includes proceedings for a declaration of title to a statutory right of occupancy.

41. An area court or a customary court or other court of equivalent jurisdiction in a state shall have jurisdiction in respect of proceedings in respect of a customary right of occupancy granted by a Local Government under this Act; and for the purposes of this paragraph, 'proceedings' include proceedings for a declaration of title to a customary right of occupancy...

The High Court Law, S.17 (1) denies original jurisdiction to the High Court in cases involving title to or interest in land "which is subject to the jurisdiction of a native court."

With reference to the instant case *(Sadikwu v. Dalori),* is the matter subject to the jurisdiction of a customary court? For an affirmative answer to be given, there must be evidence that there is a customary court that has territorial jurisdiction in the area where the land in dispute is situated . There is no evidence that there exists such a customary court. An issue that involves the ouster of a High Court's original jurisdiction can not be taken for granted: it must be proved.

The Land Tenure Law (to which S.17 (1) of the High Court Law is subject) confers jurisdiction on "native courts" where, but only where, "all parties are subject to the jurisdiction of native courts:" S. 41 (2) (a). There is no evidence that all parties in the *Sadikwu case* are subject to the jurisdiction of native courts. ("Native courts" will be replaced with "area courts" of various grades and "customary courts" in the rest of this discussion). Indeed, there is a strong indication that the 5th defendant is a Company. In a passage of the Supreme Court judgment as reported in the Nigerian Weekly Law Report, Part 447, page 160 last paragraph, G-H, there is this statement:-

> the 4th defendant averred that he neither claims any personal right or interest in the land in dispute but that he is the Managing Director of the *5th defendant which* applied for and was granted allocation of the said land by the Bornor State Ministry of Land and Survey, along Baga Road, Maiduguri, Balori Layout, followed by *issuance to it* by the same Ministry with a Certificate of a Statutory Right of Occupancy.

It is nowhere discussed in the Supreme Court judgment whether or not a company is subject to the jurisdiction of an area/customary court. The point apparently was not discussed in any of the three court proceedings the case went through. However, if it be true that the 5th defendant is a company and that companies are not subject to the jurisdiction of area/customary courts, it may be found that those courts lack jurisdiction due to "all the parties" not being subject to their jurisdiction: see the Land Tenure Law S. 41 (2) (a).

In that event, we shall have to fall back on subsection (3) of the same S. 41 (Land Tenure Law). That sub-section clearly gives jurisdiction to the High Court and the District Court (Magistrates Court) where, in like circumstances, are courts and customary courts have none. It says:-

> (3) The High Court and District Court (within the respective limits prescribed by the District Courts Law) *shall* have jurisdiction in the following proceedings:-
>
> (a) proceedings in respect of any land the subject of a statutory right of occupancy granted by a native authority or of a customary right of occupancy where one or more of the parties are not subject to the jurisdiction of native courts;

(b) proceedings of the description referred to in paragraph (a) of sub-section (2) where there is no native court of competent jurisdiction available to try the proceedings.

From S. 41 (3) (b) of the Land Tenure Law emerges another point: where there is no area/customary court of competent jurisdiction available to try the proceedings, the High Court has jurisdiction. There is no evidence discernible in the proceedings as contained in the Supreme Court judgment or in what is reported of the Court of Appeal and the High Court proceedings, that there was an area/customary court of competent jurisdiction available to try the case. Proceedings in which the appellate Courts were invited to consign our State High Courts to the limbo of moribund judicial institutions, but in which so many important questions were not raised or canvassed cannot be said to be ideal. The jurisdiction of a superior court of record should not and cannot in law be removed that way.

Both the Court of Appeal and the Supreme Court came to the conclusion that S. 41 of the Land Use Act, supported by S. 41 of the Land Tenure Law of Northern Nigeria, removed original jurisdiction from the High Court in matters relating to claims based on customary rights of occupancy or statutory rights of occupancy granted by a Local Governments or cognate authority. But did they? Let us see what those two sections actually said and from there try and find out what they did.

S. 41 of the Land Use Act (reproduced above) merely said that "An Area Court or Customary Court...shall have jurisdiction in respect of a customary right of occupancy granted by a Local Government under this Act." The jurisdiction here granted is not made exclusive. And there is nothing in the section or elsewhere in the Act that says: Wherever the area/customary court has jurisdiction, the High Court shall have none. It is humbly submitted that the legislator does not remove a court's jurisdiction in silence, but by an express provision made in clear terms. There is no such provision here in S. 41.

The Land Tenure Law of Northern Nigeria applicable in Borno State provides in S. 41 (2) that an area/customary court shall have jurisdiction in proceedings in respect of land that is subject to a statutory right of occupancy granted by a Local Government or a customary right of occupancy.

And the *High Court Law* applicable in Borno State provides in S. 17 (1) that the High Court "shall not exercise original jurisdiction in any suit or matter which, inter alia, raises any issue as to title to land or as to the title to any interest in land which is subject to the jurisdiction of an area/customary court.

From these last two provisions, the appellate courts did the simple syllogism:

> If the area/customary court has jurisdiction. The High Court does not have jurisdiction. In this case, the area/customary court has jurisdiction;

Therefore the High Court lacks jurisdiction. (Refer to the Lead Judgment at p.161, F-G commencing from "In substance...")

The point has already been made that it was not shown that any area/customary court has jurisdiction over the area concerned, or over all the parties to the action as required by statute law.

A bigger issue is that neither S. 6 (6) nor S. 236 of the 1979 Constitution was adverted to at all.

S. 6(6) vests the judicial powers of the State in the State High Court, which powers:-

> (a) Shall extend, notwithstanding anything to the contrary in this Constitution, to *all inherent powers* and sanctions of a court of law;
>
> (b) shall extend to *all matters* between persons... and to *all actions and proceedings* relating thereto, for the determination of *any question* as to the civil rights and obligations of that person.
>
> *S.236(1)* confers on a State High Court "unlimited jurisdiction to hear and determine *any* civil proceedings in which the existence or extent of a legal right, power, duty, liability, privilege, interest, obligation or claim is in issue.

The powers conferred by S. 6 (6) on State High Courts are comprehensive. Nothing is left out except those named in paragraphs (c) and (d) relating to the natural desire of the armed forces to keep their coup activities from the courts. Any diminution of these powers, it is submitted, must be made by way of a constitutional amendment or by a Decree which is said to be of equal status with the Constitution.

The jurisdiction conferred by S. 236 (1) of the 1979 Constitution is just as comprehensive. From its language, it may be added to but, in our submission, may not be detracted from except by way of a constitutional amendment or a military Decree.

It is submitted that the powers vested in the State High Courts by S. 6 (6) (a) and (b) and the jurisdiction conferred upon them by S. 236 of the 1979 Constitution cover rights and interests in land, including customary and other rights of Occupancy.

General and Specific Provisions

It may be argued that where one part of a statute makes general provisions on a subject matter and another part of the same statute makes specific provisions on the same subject matter, the specific provisions prevail. From this it may be concluded that, the 1979 Constitution and the Land Use Act being one statute, S. 6 (6) and S. 236 of the Constitution may rightly be called general provisions while S. 39 (1) and S. 41 of the Land Use Act are specific provisions regarding land matters.

This, with respect, in a misconception. The powers and jurisdictions conferred respectively by S. 6 (6) and S. 236 of the 1979 Constitution are expressed to cover all purposes for which superior courts of record (including State High Courts) are established. They vest in those courts and, unless they are duly excluded, they inhere in those courts and are exercisable by them without more. And those powers and jurisdictions, having been created and vested on the courts by the constitution, can only be excluded by the Constitution (or a military Decree, we are told.)

Now, S. 6 (6) and S. 236 of the Constitution are not on the same pedestal as S. 39 (1) and S. 41 of the Land Use Act even if the Act is a part of the Constitution. Nor are S. 39 (1) and S. 41 of the Land Use Act on the same pedestal with each other. The High Court has enough power and jurisdiction under the Constitution to entertain suits relating to rights of Occupancy, it is submitted. S. 39 (1) was found necessary simply because the legislator wanted to give the High Court *exclusive* jurisdiction which it would not have otherwise.

On the other hand, area/customary courts do not have those inherent rights and powers which the High Courts have under S. 6 (6), neither do they have the comprehensive jurisdiction which the High Courts have under S. 236 of the Constitution. They (area/customary courts) have no powers or jurisdiction except what is given them expressly by statute. In the result, S. 41 of the Land Use Act was enacted to accommodate area/customary courts, but certainly not to oust the Constitution - given powers and jurisdiction of the State High Courts.

On S.17 (1) of the High Court Law in force in Borno which purports to oust the jurisdiction of the High Court where area/customary courts have jurisdiction, it is submitted that that sub-section is contrary to S.6 (6) and S. 236 of the 1979 Constitution and so died a legal death when those sections of the Constitution came into force in 1979.

The Case of Abraham Oyeniran v. James Egbetola

A year after it dealt that deadly blow at State High Courts in the mind-buckling case of *Sadikwu v. Dalori* discussed earlier, the Supreme Court delivered its *Coup de grace* on those unfortunate courts. The occasion was the delivery of the judgment in the case of *Abraham Oyeniran and 3 others v. James Egbetola and another* (1997) 5 NWLR (Part 504) 122. There again, the issue arose whether the Osun High Court had jurisdiction to entertain a claim to the right of occupancy over a piece of land in the rural parts of Iwo East Local Government Area. The Court of Appeal had held that the High Court had jurisdiction. The Supreme Court, relying on an *obiter dictum* of the erudite Karibi-Whyte J.S.C. in *Baba Bakin Salati v. Tale Shehu* (1986) 1 NWLR (Part 15) 198, and the unanimous decision of the Supreme Court itself in *Sadikwu v. Dalori* held that the High Court had no jurisdiction in the matter. The dictum of the Hon. Justice Karibi-Whyte in *Salati v. Shehu* which the Supreme Court refereed to in *Oyeniran v. Egbetola* reads:

> S.39 (1) of the Land Use Act) specifically relates to "proceedings in respect of any land subject of a statutory right of occupancy granted by the Military Governor or deemed to be granted..." On the other hand Section 41 confers jurisdiction on Area Courts or Customary Courts or Courts of equivalent jurisdiction in respect of customary right of occupancy granted by a Local Government under this Act. There is no ambiguity in the two sections that the exclusive original jurisdiction in respect of land held under statutory right of occupancy is vested in the High Court of the State, whereas jurisdiction in respect of customary right of occupancy is vested in the Area

or Customary Courts. The exercise of these jurisdiction will seem to me mutually exclusive: There is no doubt therefore that the one cannot exercise the jurisdiction of the other." (Parenthesis supplied).

n the lead judgment in *Oyeniran v. Egetola,* Mohammed J.S.C. said: "I have looked into the provisions of S. 41 of the Land Use Act 1978 and, in my respectful view, I will interpret it in the same way as ny learned brothers, Karibi-Whyte J.S.C. and Wali J.S.C. had done."

He then went on to account for the absence of the term "exclusive" n S. 41, in these words:

"The word 'exclusive" which the lower court pointed out to have been omitted in S. 41 of the Land Use Act 1978 could not fit into the definition of the provisions of the section.

The rule of interpretation is that the Act must be read as a whole in order to understand its ordinary meaning..." (P. 131).

He gave further explanation and supporting argument in the following words:

> Since the jurisdiction to determine proceedings in respect of Customary Right of Occupancy is shared between Area Courts, Customary Courts or other courts of equivalent jurisdiction, the word 'exclusive' cannot fit into the provisions of S. 41 of the Land Use Act 1978" (P. 131).

With profound respect and trepidation, one begs to state that the reason for omitting the term "exclusive" from S. 41 is not the drafting problem of using that term in a provision that gives jurisdiction to more courts than one. That problem can easily be overcome in a provision like this:

> the Area Court, the Customary Court and other courts of equivalent jurisdiction shall, to the exclusion of all other courts, have jurisdiction in respect of proceedings regarding customary rights of occupancy..

It is not therefore that the draftsman could not properly insert the idea of exclusiveness into S. 41, but that the legislator did not intend to confer exclusive jurisdiction on the courts mentioned in that section. We shall came back to this later.

It is the view of the Supreme Court that the Land Use Act Classified land in each State into two, urban and non-urban, and assigned jurisdiction in respect of urban land to State High Courts, and jurisdiction in respect of non-urban land to Area Courts,

Customary Courts and courts of equivalent jurisdiction. Uwais J.S.C. (as he then was) so held in *Salati v. Shehu* in these words:

> now the division of jurisdiction of the courts established in a State in respect of land matters is contained in sections 39, 40 and 41 of the Land Use Act 1978. The division appears to follow the classification of land into urban areas and non-urban areas

In the instant case *(Oyeniran v. Egbetola),* Mohammed J.S.C. said at page 132:

> prior to the enactment of the Land Use Act, in 1978, both High Courts and the Customary Courts in Oyo State had unlimited jurisdiction in land matters. The Customary Courts were however made to apply the customary law of the place where the land was situated. There was then no classification of land holdings as has now been done in the Land Use Act 1978.The present classification has assigned jurisdiction to a hierarchy of courts based on the location of the land the subject matter in dispute.

The Argument appears water-tight. It is, however, submitted with respect, that jurisdiction under the Land Use Act is not intended to follow the suggested urban-rural divide at all. Section 5 (1) of the Act provides as follows:

> 5(1) It shall be lawful for the Governor in respect of land, *whether or not in an urban area,*—
>
> (a) to grant statutory rights of occupancy to any person for all purposes." (Emphasis supplied).

Therefor where the Governor grants a statutory right of occupancy over land in a non-urban area, jurisdiction in disputes concerning such land shall be exclusively in the State High Court under S. 39 (1) which merely speaks of -:

> any land the subject of a statutory right of occupancy granted by the Governor or deemed to be granted by him under this Act,

Without making any reference to the geographical location of the land in question.

When the Supreme Court said that a statute must be read as a whole in order to understand its ordinary meaning (lead judgment, P. 131), one could not agree more. However, it is suggested with humility that since the Land Use Act is part of the 1979 Constitution, the scheme of the Constitution regarding the powers and jurisdictions of our courts over civil matters should be studied with a view to solving the problem posed by S. 39 (1) and S. 41 of the Land Use Act. As previously indicated, S. 6 of the 1979 Constitution vests the judicial powers of the Federation and of the States in the Superior Courts of record established for the Federation and for the States respectively (see S. 6 (1) and 6(2). These are the Supreme Court, the Court of Appeal, the Federal High Court, a State High Court, a Sharia Court of Appeal of a State, a Customary Court of Appeal of a State, and such other courts as may be established by the Federal and State legislatures (see S. 6(5). Section 6(6) (a) and (b) vests these courts with what can only be described as universal powers over matters in dispute.

Section 236(1) of the same Constitution vests State High Courts with what is also universal jurisdiction over matters, civil and criminal, subject only to the Constitution itself, when it provides thus:

> *236(1)* subject to the provisions of this Constitution and in addition to such other jurisdiction as may be conferred upon it by law, the High Court of a State shall have *unlimited* jurisdiction to hear and determine *any civil proceedings* in which the existence or extent of a legal right, power, duty, liability, privilege, interest, obligation or claim is in issue..." (Emphasis supplied.)

This blanket jurisdiction may be added to, but there is no provision that it may be cut down. Again, the words "unlimited" and "to hear and determine any civil proceedings" appear to make the jurisdiction of State High Courts not only unlimited in scope but also universal in application as regards subject matter.

If the above interpretation of S. 6(6) (a) and (b) and of S. 236(1) is correct, not only the State High Courts but also other superior courts of record have unrestricted judicial powers over all matters in issue except where the Constitution says otherwise.

That explains why the Constitution is careful to exclude other courts in appropriate cases. For example, why else was it found necessary to provide in S. 213 of the Constitution:

"The Supreme Court shall have jurisdiction *to the exclusion of any other court of law in Nigeria* to hear and determine appeals from the Court of Appeal," despite Nigeria's clear hierarchy of courts? Why was it found necessary to provide as follows in S. 219:

> subject to the provisions of this Constitution, the Court of Appeal shall have jurisdiction, *to the exclusion of any other court of law in Nigeria,* to

hear and determine appeals from the Federal High Court, High Court of a State, Sharia Court of Appeal of a State and Customary Court of Appeal of a State?

Ridiculous as the suggestion may be, it is not just to abolish appeals to the Privy Council in U.K. that the Constitution provides that from any determination of the Supreme Court, no appeal shall lie to any other body or person: S.215. For the same reason, the Constitution found it necessary to set a limit to the appellate jurisdiction of the Sharia Court of Appeal and the Customary Court of Appeal in S. 242 and 247 respectively.

At the other end of the ladder, courts of law which are not superior courts of record have no jurisdiction at all except what is conferred on them by the statutes that create them. This is because, unlike the superior courts of record which derive their jurisdictions from both the Constitution and the statutes that create them, these "minor" courts depend solely on their creators.

The rationale for the enactment of S.39 and S.41 of the Land Use Act has hopefully become clear. Section 39 is there to keep off other superior courts of record from exercising original jurisdiction in matters concerning statutory rights of occupancy granted or deemed to be granted by a State Governor. This those other courts could do, in our submission, but for the provisions of S. 39 (1). Section 41 of the Act is there to let in Area Courts and Customary Courts where customary rights of occupancy are in issue. They would have no jurisdiction otherwise, and it was considered convenient to let litigants resort to them, if they so desire, since lands subject to customary rights of occupancy are found in large numbers in areas where those courts exists.

This, in our submission, accounts for S. 39 (1) and S. 41 of the Land Use Act, not any desire to follow a classification of land into urban and non-urban, the High Courts taking care of urban land matters and Area/Customary Courts catering for non-urban land.

As already pointed out, a large number of statutory rights of occupancy are granted by State Governors in non-urban areas, especially where such land is acquired for industrial and large scale farming purposes. And land covered by a Governor's statutory right of occupancy is subject to the jurisdiction of State High Courts, its non-urban location notwithstanding: See S.5(1) (a) and S. 39(1) of the Land Use Act.

It is submitted that the effects of ousting the jurisdiction of State High Courts in matters involving customary rights of occupancy will be far-reaching and unwholesome. First, the Area Courts and Customary Courts will be innundated with land matters, some of them quite intricate. Many, perhaps most, of these Courts cannot read or understand survey plans. Land cases will therefore be done without plans, as they were in the 1930's and 1940's by the Native Courts. So judgments will not be tied to plans. Years later, those who lost land cases will reopen them, claiming that the lands they lost were kilometres away from their current claims.

Secondly, Sharia and Customary Courts of Appeal will be overwhelmed by appeals. Also a number of States do not have Customary Courts of Appeal. In such places, the Magistrate and District Courts will be jammed with appeals in addition to their normal overdose of criminal cases. One wonders how a magistrate or his counterpart in the District Court, persons who are trained lawyers, could be expected to do appeal cases on land without plans.

Thirdly, State High Courts will lose a large portion of their legal business and the Judges may become disillusioned. Lawyers will lose their main source of legal fees. Society generally will be the worse for the change.

One therefore hopes that the Supreme Court will see its way clear to distinguish the two decisions and restore original jurisdiction to the State High Courts.

In the alternative, the Federal Attorney-General may wish to take advantage of the current military rule to effect necessary amendments to the Land Use Act or the Constitution, as that will be an uphill task if civil rule returns. Already State High Courts are full of "preliminary objections" based on absence of original jurisdiction on the part of those Courts in land cases. Unsuccessful litigants are suitably amending their grounds of appeal to reflect their objection to the assumption of original jurisdiction by State High Courts. The pandora's box has been opened inadvertently by the Supreme Court.

The social disadvantages of the change appear considerable and may get more uncomfortable as time goes on. One wonders what the benefits are, or are likely to be. And so, where do we go from here.

Notes

1. *Abubakar Sadikwu v. Alhaji Abba Dalori* (1996) 4 KLR (Pt 40) 796
2. (Cap 59), Laws of Northern Nigeria, 1963 (Applicable to Bornor State)
3. (Cap 49) Laws of Northern Nigeria, 1963 (Applicable for Bornor State)
4. (1986) 2 NWLR (Pt 24) 560, 572-73
5. (1997) 11 S.C. 77
6. (1962) ALLNLR 1 at p. 7
7. (1996) NWLR (Pp 447) 158-9
8. (1968) 1 ALL NLR 1 at p.8
9. (1986) 1 S.C. 332; (1986) 1 1 NWLR (Pt 15) 198
10. (1996) NWLR (Pt 447) 159-160 (Emphasis supplied) See (1996) 4 KLR at Pp 801-802
11. (Cap.59) Laws of Northern Nigeria, 1963 (Applicable to Bornor State
12. (1986) ALL NLR 53; (1986) 1 NWLR (Pt 15) 198-211, particularly at p.61
13. (1996) 4 KLR (Pt 40) at Pp: 805-807
14. (Emphasis supplied)
15. ("Native Courts" will be replaced with "area courts" of various grades and "Customary Courts" in the rest of this discussion)
16. See (1996) NWLR (Part 447) Page 160, paragraphs G-H
17. (Refer to the leading judgment at P. 161, F-G. Commencing from "In substance...")
18. (1997) 5 NWLR (Part 504) 122
19. (1986) 1 NWLR (Part 15) 198
20. (Parenthesis supplied)
21. See, p. 131
22. See p. 131
23. At p. 132
24. (Emphasis supplied)
25. See page 131 of the leading judgment\
26. (Emphasis supplied)

CHAPTER 3

Offences And Penalties Under The Failed Banks Decree: An Appraisal

By

Prof. C.O. Okonkwo S.A.N., Dean, Faculty of Law University of Nigeria

Introduction

Nigeria has gone through very turbulent times which have affected all spheres of life. Worse hit is the economy. And banks are central to the economy. Fraud, corruption and mismanagement have wrecked the economy and these have sent many banks crashing[1]. Statistics from the Nigerian Deposit Insurance Corporation show that between 1990 and 1994 banks recorded a total of 6 billion naira fraud. Actual and expected losses to the banks is estimated at 1.4 billion naira. Even at that these figures are considered gross underestimate of the true position because "many banks had reneged in rendering the required returns on frauds" to the Nigerian Deposit Insurance Corporation[2]. There are obvious reasons why bank frauds should attract utmost attention and drastic remedies.

Apart from various regulatory devices which have been established from time to time, some statutes contain provisions devoted specifically to these problems. These can be found in the Banks and other Financial Institutions Decree 1991, the Central Bank of Nigeria Decree 1991, The Nigerian Deposit Insurance Corporation Act 1988[3] and the repealed Banking Act 1969[4]. These are in addition to relevant offences in the Criminal Code and in the Companies and Allied Matters Act 1990[5].

Notwithstanding these regulatory attempts malpractices continued to thrive resulting in the recent collapse or near collapse of many banks and financial institutions. It was clear that the problem called for something direct and drastic. In the military fashion this should involve a decree dealing directly and specifically with the problem in hand, removal of adjudication from the ordinary courts to special tribunals, dispensation with some traditional rules of evidence and procedure, speedy trial of cases and severity of punishment. Accordingly the failed banks (Recovery of Debts) and Financial Malpractices in banks Decree (No.18) 1994 was promulgated. The Decree has been amended by No.18 of 1995 Decree.

The Decree establishes the Failed Banks (Recovery of Debts) and Financial Malpractices in Banks Tribunal[6] which is charged with the responsibility of recovering debts owed to a failed bank arising in the ordinary course of business and which remain outstanding as at the date the bank is closed or declared a failed bank by the Central Bank of Nigeria. The Tribunal has power to try offences created by the Decree, by the Banks and Other financial Institutions Decree 1991, the Nigerian Deposit Insurance Corporation Decree 1988 and other offences relating to the business or operation of a bank under any enactment[7]. The Decree contains some special rules of evidence and procedure for recovering debts owed to failed banks[8].

Schedule 1 to the Decree deals with the procedure for recovery of debts at the Tribunal and the appendix contains specimen Forms. Schedule 2 deals with the procedure for the trial of offences before the Tribunal while the appendix also deals with applicable Forms. Offences and penalties, with which this paper is concerned, are dealt with in Part III of the Decree.

2. Offences And Penalties

Section 19 of the Decree creates a wide range of offences designed, *inter alia* to catch the usual form of banking malpractice at the highest level. These consist of the offences of knowingly, recklessly etc granting, approving a loan, advance etc to any person:

1(i) Without adequate security or collateral;
(ii) With no security or collateral;
(iii) With defective security or collateral;
(iv) Without perfecting a security or collateral obtained;
2. Granting or approving a loan etc above the officers limit

3. Granting or approving a loan etc in contravention of any law or regulation
4. Receiving or participating in sharing of a bribe in connection with a loan etc
5. Recklessly granting a loan or interest waiver to a solvent debtor
6. Bank's debtor or customer willfully or negligently giving false information to it.

We shall now examine these offences in some detail.

2.1 Loan Granted With Inadequate Security Or Collateral (Section 19(1)(a)(i))

By section 19(1)(a)(1) any director, manager, officer or employee of a bank who knowingly, recklessly, negligently, willfully or otherwise is connected with the grant or approval of a loan, an advance, a guarantee or any other credit facility or financial accommodation to any person, without adequate security or collateral, contrary to the accepted practice or the bank's regulations, is guilty of an offence under the Decree.

If a bank takes adequate security for a loan granted by it, the risk of loss hardly exists. Any prudent businessman dealing with his own money, must take such security. It is therefore breach of trust and criminal misconduct to willfully or negligently put other people's money at risk in breach of accepted norms. The offence may be committed by any director, officer or employee of a bank and may be committed collectively by the board. Where an inadequately secured loan is granted by an officer, his superior who is in a position of authority, who is cognisant of the transaction and who fails to prevent it may equally be guilty of aiding the offence[9] or of failing to stop it[10].

Where such loan is granted by the board, every director present at the board meeting at which approval was granted, is guilty of this offence unless he proves that he dissented from the decision of the board and took reasonable steps to prevent its implementation.

The mental element of this offence is established if it is shown that the errant director or officer had knowledge that the loan is inadequately secured. That he did not support or approve of it is immaterial. Likewise if he acted willfully. It will therefore be immaterial that the manager was "directed from above" to grant the loan. Recklessness or negligence will also suffice as a mental element. Recklessness encompasses negligence and involves a higher decree of culpability. Recklessness will attract heavier penalty than negligence.

A security will be deemed inadequate if when realised the yield is less than the total sum due under the loan agreement. But adequacy will be judged as at the time of the loan. If at that time the value of the security was adequate but subsequent events render it inadequate, no offence is committed unless there was negligence in failing to foresee such supervening inadequacy. Put differently, knowledge of the inadequacy of the security or negligence in relation thereto, must exist at the time of the loan agreement.

2.2 Loan Granted With No Security Or Collateral (Section 19(1)(1)(ii).

While under the previous head security is taken but is inadequate, under the present head, no security whatsoever is taken. The latter is a more reprehensible state of affairs than the former but they are subject to the same penalty.[11]

2.3 Loan Granted With A Defective Security Or Collateral

Although this offence may be committed knowingly or willfully, the more usual case will be where it is committed negligently. The bank official through some carelessness fails to observe some defect in the security.

2.4 Loan Granted Without Perfecting A Security Or Collateral Obtained

Deliberate or willful failure by a bank officer to perfect a security will clearly involve collusion with the customer and evidently criminal conduct. It is doubtful whether criminality should attach where the omission is merely negligent (as distinct from reckless in the traditional sense). Generally, negligence as a basis of criminal liability applies to offences which are not of a very serious nature. The offence here is punishable with imprisonment for five years without option of a fine. One can hardly think of a negligent offence for which imprisonment is the only penalty. Perhaps the justification here is the devastating effect which the ever increasing rate of bank frauds has had on the banking sector and the economy.

2.5 Bank Officer Granting Loan Above His Limit (Section 19(1)(b))

By Section 19(1)(b), any director, manager, officer or employee of a bank who grants, approves the grant or is otherwise connected with the grant or approval of a loan, an advance, a guarantee or any other credit facility which is above his limit as laid down by law or any regulatory authority or the bank's regulations is guilty of an offence under the Decree.

This, again, is one of the malpractices frequently encountered in ailing banks. Managers sometimes deliberately exceed their authorised limits hoping that the loan will be repaid before the misconduct is noticed or just brazenly in obvious defiance of the rules.

There can be no question of a bank executive not knowing his authorised lending limit. Such an incredible assertion will at least exhibit recklessness or negligence either of which suffices for criminal liability. This kind of defence was reportedly put forward recently by the chief executive of a bank described as technically distressed. The chairman of the bank in his comments to the Central Bank of Nigeria said:

> It is difficult to believe that the managing director of a bank does not know the true lending limit of the bank he is managing especially having been an executive director of the same bank for several years before, being appointed as managing director. Any claim of such ignorance, in my opinion, amounts to gross dishonesty[12]."

2.6 Loan Granted In Contravention Of Any Law, Regulation Etc. (Section 19(1)(c).

It is an offence under this head for a director or bank official to grant, approve the grant or otherwise be connected with the grant or approval of a loan, an advance, a guarantee or any other credit facility to any person in contravention of any law for the time being in force, any regulation, circular, or procedure as laid down from time to time, by the regulatory authorities or by the bank. Relevant regulatory rules may be found *inter alia,* in the Banks and Other Financial Institutions Decree 1991, the Central Bank of Nigeria Decree 1991 and the Nigerian Deposit Insurance Corporation Act 1988. The Central Bank also issues guidelines from time to time as do various banks to their staff. To act in contravention of these is an offence.

The alternatives contained in this provision may raise problems of interpretation where there is inconsistency between the provisions/contents of a law, regulation, circular or procedure laid down by a bank or a regulatory authority. It seems obvious that where a loan complies with an existing law but is in contravention of a regulation or circular laid down by any regulatory authority or by the bank, no offence is committed. The law is superior to such regulation or circular.

This, however, may sometimes only be technically justifiable. If a rule of law is found no longer conducive to good banking, breach of a corrective guideline issued by the Central Bank before the law is amended may rightly be held punishable, at least, if bad faith is shown. As between conflicting circulars issued by a regulatory authority and a bank, the former will prevail. Activity which complies with the former but not with the latter, will not be penalised. As between two conflicting circulars/guidelines issued by the same authority, the later in time will prevail.

2.7 Receiving Benefit Towards Or After The Procurement Of A Loan (Section 19(1)(d).

By Section 19(1)(d), any director, manager, officer or employee of a bank who receives or participates in sharing, for personal gratification, any money, profit, property or pecuniary benefit towards or after the procurement of a loan, an advance, a guarantee or any other credit facility from any person whether or not that person is a customer of the bank is guilty of an offence.

This provision deals with the offence of corruption by bank officials. Like the offence of corruption in the Criminal Code[13] it is immaterial that the benefit is unsolicited and is given after the loan, advance etc had been given. The expression "for personal gratification" restricts the scope of the offence to benefit received by the bank official himself. It does not extend, for example, to benefit conferred on a member of his family[14]. Under the Criminal Code the offence of corruption is committed even if the property or benefit is demanded or received for "any other person[15]." The equivalent offence in Section 43 of the Banks and Other Financial institutions Decree 1991 is committed if the bank official receives a reward for his own personal benefit or advantage or for that of any of his personal benefit or advantage or for that of any of his relations.

Again, under the Criminal Code and under the BOFID the offence of corruption is committed even if no property, benefit etc is received. It is enough if the offender corruptly asks or agrees to receive the property or benefit. Under the present offence the bribe must have been received or shared.

There is no justification for restricting the scope of this offence. As with the Criminal Code and the BOFID it should cover situations where a bank official merely asks for or agrees to take a benefit and to cases where the benefit is not for the official himself but for someone else.

2.8 Recklessly Granting Or Approving Loan Or Interest Waiver (Section 19(1)(e)).

It is an offence under the Decree for any director, manager, officer or employee of a bank to recklessly grant or approve a loan or an interest waiver where the borrower is known to have the ability to repay the loan and interest[16]. The expression "where the borrower is known to have the ability to repay" refers to knowledge of persons other than the bank official who grants the waiver. If he himself has the requisite knowledge and nevertheless grants the waiver, his conduct is deliberate, not reckless. The provision envisages a situation where in granting a waiver, the officer is reckless in not discovering that the borrower has ability to repay.

It does not, of course, mean that no offence is committed where the officer who approves a loan or an interest waiver has knowledge that the borrower has ability to pay. Although not specifically covered, such conduct is an offence under this head on the ground that where a less reprehensible mental element is prescribed for an offence, that offence may, *a fortiori,* be committed by an even more reprehensible mental element of the same kind[17].

2.9 Debtor Or Customer Of A Bank Giving False Information (Section 19(2))

Any person who is indebted to or who is a customer of a bank, and who negligently, willfully or recklessly makes a written or oral statement, or gives any information, or fills any form to a bank knowing it to be false, fake, non-existent or fictitious with the intention of concealing his identity from the bank in order to avoid the repayment of a loan, an advance, a guarantee or any other credit facility granted him by the bank is guilty of an offence under Section 19(2) of the Decree. If the offender is a body corporate, any of its directors, managers, officers, employees or partners who is responsible or is in any way connected with the doing of any of the forbidden acts is guilty of the same offence and is liable to the same punishment[18].

In the case of a body corporate, the director, employee etc who is connected with the offence must have the same guilty knowledge as the principal offender.

Curiously this offence is not as wide as it should be or as is presumably intended by the lawmaker. Being confined as it is, to a customer or person indebted to a bank, its tentacles would not catch a guarantor who by misinformation seeks to conceal his identity. The offender must be a customer of, or be indebted to the bank, at the time of the misinformation. A guarantor is none of these. The offence will be more far-reaching if the opening part was expanded to include "any person who in connection with any loan, advance, credit facility by a bank, or being a customer of a bank, negligently, willfully or recklessly" does any of the forbidden things.

2.1.0 Non Compliance With A Repayment Order

A person commits an offence if he fails to comply with an order of the Tribunal under Section 13(2) for the payment of loan and interest within the time specified in an order under that section. This offence was introduced by the Failed Banks (Recovery of Debts) and Financial Malpractices in Banks (Amendment) Decree No.18 of 1995.

3. Conviction For Attempt Or Full Offence When Disclosed But Not Charged

If a person is charged with any of the above offences and the evidence discloses merely an attempt to commit the offence, he may be convicted of the attempt even though he is not charged with that offence[19]. Likewise, if he is charged with an attempt and the evidence discloses commission of the full offence, he may be convicted of the full offence[20].

4. Complicity

If a tribunal trying an offence under this Decree is satisfied that a person who has not been charged before it, acted in concert or conspired with any person, or knowingly participated to any extent whatsoever in the commission of the offence, the tribunal has power to treat that person in like manner as a person charged before it, notwithstanding anything to the contrary in any other enactment[21]. This means that it may have the person charged and tried before it.

More directly, it is provided in Section 23(4) that any person who aids, abets, counsels, procures or conspires with any other person to commit any of the offences in the Decree is guilty of the offence and liable to the same punishment as is prescribed for that offence.

By Section 22(1), where an offence under the Decree is committed by a body corporate and is proved to have been committed with the connivance of or to be attributable to any neglect on the part of a director, manager, secretary or other similar officer, or any person purporting to act in any such capacity, he as well as the body corporate where practicable are deemed to be guilty of that offence.

5.1 Penalties

Section 20 of the Decree deals with penalties for the offences created in Section 19[22]. Imprisonment is mandatory for all the offences. There is no option of a fine. All offences involving the willful, reckless or negligent granting of a loan, an advance etc, (i.e sections 19(1)(a),(b) and (c) are punishable with a maximum of five years imprisonment[23].

Receiving gratification in connection with a loan, an advance etc, is punishable with imprisonment for three years. The penalty here is considered quite low. The offence of corruption under the Criminal Code is punishable with imprisonment for seven years where the administration of justice is not affected and fourteen years where it is affected[24].

The offence of recklessly granting a loan or an interest waiver where the debtor has ability to repay is punishable with imprisonment for three years. So also is the offence of giving false information to a bank in order to avoid repayment of a loan. The offence of non compliance with repayment order is punishable with imprisonment for a term not exceeding three years without option of a fine.

The maximum terms of imprisonment prescribed for these offences seem generally quite low considering the widespread nature of these offences, the brazen manner in which they are often committed, the magnitude and widespread nature of the consequences to the bank and its customers, the fact that they are committed by persons in a position of trust, and the realisation that maximum sentences are as a rule reserved for persistent offenders and offences of the worst kind in that class of offence.

Imprisonment without option of a fine seems appropriate for banking malpractices committed willfully and perhaps recklessly. It is improper that discretion to impose a fine should be taken away in respect of offences of negligence.

5.2 Punishment For Attempts

An attempt to commit any of the offences discussed above carries the same punishment prescribed for the full offence[25]. Naturally the courts will bear in mind in sentencing, that more punishment is deserved where the full offence has been committed than where there is only an attempt,[26] and more relevantly where the person making the attempt desisted of his own free will from completing the offence[27].

5.3 Punishment Where Offence Is Committed By A Body Corporate

A body corporate may commit any of the offences contained in the Decree. But as imprisonment without option of a fine is the major penalty, and as a corporation cannot be imprisoned, that punishment is inappropriate. However, as we have scen, a director, manager, secretary or other officer with whose connivance or by whose neglect the offence is committed may be guilty[28]. For the corporation itself, a more drastic penalty is provided.

By Section 22(2), if a body corporate other than a bank, is convicted of an offence under the Decree, the tribunal may order that the body corporate be wound up and the body corporate shall, without any further assurance than that order, be wound up. In that event all its assets, after satisfying all claims of the receiver or liquidator shall be forfeited to the Federal Government.

This is a most extreme penalty - an imposition of capital punishment on the body corporate. This, presumably, is necessitated by the fact that there is no option of a fine for the offences created by the Decree. It is suggested however that a fine, should have been prescribed for offending bodies corporate. Clearly the offence would, in every case, have been committed by the human agents of the body corporate and they would be liable to imprisonment. The corporation itself should therefore be liable to some less drastic punishment. Secondly, the offences created by the Decree are not so very serious as to justify the extinction of a convicted body corporate.

Worse still, is the forfeiture of the assets of the body corporate. Such forfeiture may amount to the forfeiture of the interests of individual shareholders for an offence committed by their directors unknown to them. There is no justification for this.

It is believed that the tribunal will invoke this penalty only in the most extreme cases, for example, where there is fraud in the object of the corporation or where its continued existence is against public interest.

6. Personal liability Of Directors Etc For Irrecoverable Loan (s.16).

By Section 16(1) if the information and details on the security pledged for a loan filed before the Tribunal are impossible to locate, or no security is pledged at all, or the debtors identity is difficult to locate or he is found to be non-existent, fake, fictitious or unidentifiable, the Tribunal shall hold liable, for the outstanding loan and interest, the directors, shareholders, partners, managers, officers and other employees of the failed bank who in the performance of their duties were found to have been connected in any way with the granting of the loan which has become irrevocable. Liability is joint and several[29]. Thee is a defence if it is shown to the satisfaction of the Tribunal that the debt was incurred without the consent of the director, partner, shareholder, manager, officer or employee or that he exercised all such diligence as he ought to have exercised having regard to the nature of his functions and all the circumstances of the case[30].

7.1 **Confiscation Or Surrender Of Property** (Section 20(2-5)

Where a person s convicted of an offence under the Decree or any other law, the Tribunal may order confiscation of his property, moveable or immovable, of a value equal to the amount involved in the offence or of such other value as the Tribunal may deem fair and just in the circumstance[31]. The convicted person may voluntarily surrender moveable or immovable property of a value equal to the amount involved in the offence or of such other value as he may decide[32].

Confiscated or surrendered property shall be forfeited to the bank that suffered the loss, or in the case of a failed bank, to the receiver or liquidator for the bank's benefit, or to such other person, as in the opinion of the Tribunal, deserves to be compensated for loss suffered[33].

7.2 **Mitigation Of Penalty**

If confiscation or voluntary surrender of property results in full or substantial recovery of the amount involved in the offence, the Tribunal may, if it deems it equitable, reduce or decline to impose the penalty specified in Section 20(1). This provision of Section 20(5) needs close scrutiny. Ordinarily, the fact that the money stolen or misappropriated has been restored is a strong mitigating factor34. Section 20(5) therefore gives the Tribunal a discretion to reduce or decline to impose the stipulated penalty if confiscation or voluntary surrender of property resuits in full or substantial recovery and the Tribunal considers it equitable to exercise its discretion under the subsection. Exercise of the discretion not to impose any sentence at all does not obviously dispense with the duty to pronounce a verdict of guilty of the offence charged before applying the discretion. This was decided by the Special Appeal Tribunal in *Federal Republic of Nigeria v. Mallam S. Bello Abubakar* (popularly known as the Gamji Bank Case).

Section 20(5) grants mitigation to an offender if property is recovered by confiscation or voluntary surrender. Obviously voluntary surrender will attract greater sympathy than confiscation. Voluntary surrender shows or is consistent with remorse which is a strong mitigating factor[35]. And full recovery deserves greater mitigation than substantial recovery. In every case a most important consideration is the manner in which the offence was committed. If it involves breach of trust (an aggravating factor in sentencing or serious fraud, even full recovery may not warrant outright exemption from punishment. Custodial sentence may be imperative. However in some cases where there is full or substantial recovery of the amount involved in the offence but the offence is not of a fraudulent nature, a court may be inclined to impose a fine. Unfortunately, however, this option is not available as punishment for offences under the Decree. The Tribunal is thus left with no half-way measure between outright impunity and imprisonment. Yet cases will occur which deserve some half-way measure. For this reason it is suggested that Section 20(5) should be amended to include the alternative of fine whenever the discretion in the subsection is exercised. An example of a situation in which a fine may be desirable is where there is substantial recovery in respect of a negligent as distinct from a fraudulent offence and the offender derived no benefit from the commission of the offence.

An overriding consideration in exercising the discretion in Section 20(5) is that the Tribunal must deem it *equitable* to do so. Ordinarily higher tribunals do not disturb the exercise of discretion by lower ones. They do so however if the exercise of discretion is arbitrary or has proceeded on wrong principles, if irrelevant considerations have been taken into account or if it is not exercised judicially[36].

In the Gamji Bank Case the lower Tribunal declined to impose the penalty prescribed for the offence charged because "the accused has completely repaid the sum of N57,585,226.00 involved in the crime as stated in counts 20, 21 and 22 of the charge[37]." It stated that it was doing so under Section 20(5) but did not indicate expressly or impliedly that it considered it equitable to do so or the reasons for so considering it. It did of course give reasons for resorting to Section 20(5).[38] The Appeal Tribunal held that the lower Tribunal was in error in its application of the subsection because it "did not direct its mind directly or by necessary implication to the factor having the principal relevance" in the matter, namely the equitable consideration. Consequently, it held, the discretion had not been exercised judicially or judiciously. It also held that the factors outlined by the lower Tribunal[39] for resorting to Section 20(5) did not relate to the degree of the defendant's culpability for the offence committed by him nor did they constitute redeeming features for the offences which the Appeal Tribunal described as "outright theft of a colossal sum of money belonging to a bank[40]." Having adverted to the serious adverse effects which such acts have on the economy and the banking industry, the Appeal Tribunal went on to say that the defendant's act was all the more

> reprehensible because it was committed by one to whom the money was entrusted for management. The turpitude of the defendant in stealing the moneys of his employers Gamji Bank Plc, in the manner he did stares everybody in the face. The turpitude remains, notwithstanding the fact that he has more or less refunded the amount involved in the charge.
>
> This, therefore, in our judgment, is not a case where it can be properly said that one considers it equitable not to impose a sentence. In our judgment, a custodial sentence alone, can meet the justice of this case and serve as a deterrent to the class of the defendant, in the banking industry, with an inclination to help themselves to the money of the bank in their care and custody. One of the mischiefs the Decree is aimed at is the subject matter of this case. Inadequate punishment will defeat the object.
>
> The fact that the defendant has refunded in full the amount involved in the charge will certainly go in mitigation of sentence. In our judgment, it will be equitable to do so, for it is a redeeming feature of the case[41]."

The Tribunal imposed a concurrent sentence of 3 years imprisonment out of a prescribed maximum of 7 years on each of the counts on which the accused was convicted.

It is difficult to criticise the sentence imposed by the Appeal Tribunal in this case because the aggravating factors far outweigh the only mitigating factor (refund) and policy considerations weigh in favour of the Appeal Tribunal's approach. The disparity in sentencing approach between the appellate and lower tribunals is remarkable and highlights the need for consistent sentencing practices in our courts.

7.3. The Amount Involved In The Offence

This expression is quite problematic. It is relevant both to mitigation of sentence and to the grant of bail. If there is full recovery of "the amount involved in the offence" sentence may be mitigated. And a Tribunal may grant bail to a person charged with an offence for an amount equal to that "involved in the offence" if he deposits half of that amount as security for bail, provides surety for the balance and deposits his passport with the Tribunal. This is provided in Section 26. The expression is also relevant to confiscation under Section 20(2).

The problem is how to determine the amount involved in an offence. In straightforward cases where the substance of the charge is that D has taken or converted the bank's money to his own use or to the use of another, no problem arises. It is money which he should repay and so the total amount taken or outstanding is the amount involved in the offence. If D a bank manager without authorisation lends N50,000,000 of the bank's money to his private company and it is repaid even before the transaction is detected, this is stealing[42]. If he is subsequently charged with that offence is the N50,000,000 the amount involved in the offence? The answer is obviously yes. For the purpose of Section 20(5) the Tribunal may grant remission if it considers it equitable to do so. But for the purpose of Section 26 a problem arises because D must deposit half the amount involved in the offence before he is granted bail. It will be absurd to require him to deposit any part of the money which had already been repaid in full. It is submitted therefore that reference to the amount involved in the offence means any part of the amount involved in the offence which has not been repaid.

More difficult are cases in which the offender did not and could not have benefitted from the amount involved in the offence and would not ordinarily be expected to refund it. In such cases the amount involved in the offence, it is suggested, should not be taken into account for purposes of mitigation of penalty under Section 20(5) or confiscation of property under Section 20(2) or of bail under Section 26. The reason for this is that the policy of the provisions is to recover the sums unlawfully taken from the bank by the offender or lost to the bank through his default. If this necessity does not exist the yardstick of the amount "involved in the offence" should not apply.

It is submitted that the discretion in Section 20(5) will apply to offences which carry a mandatory minimum term of imprisonment such as Section 2(1)(a) of the Exchange Control (Anti-Sabotage) Act 1984 (Cap 114). There are at least two reasons for this. The first is that the Failed Banks Decree is later in time than the Exchange Control Act. Secondly, it will be contrary to the spirit of Section 20(5) to impose a mandatory minimum term of imprisonment despite full voluntary surrender of the amount involved in the offence.

8. An Issue Of Jurisdiction

One issue of jurisdiction which evoked debate but which now appears settled touches on the jurisdiction of the Tribunal to try offences not contained in banking or banking related legislation. Specifically Section 3 of the Failed Banks (Recovery of Debt and Financial Malpractices in Banks) Decree provides that the Tribunal has power to try offences in some designated statutes and also by paragraph 3(d) to "try other offences relating to the business or operation of a bank under any enactment." The debate was whether the Tribunal could by reason of this omnibus provision try an offence in the Criminal or Penal Code of a State if its commission (and not the definition of the offence) related to a bank. If an officer of a bank stole money belonging to the bank he would ordinarily be charged with stealing under the Criminal or Penal Code of the State where the offence occured and in the courts of that state. The critical issue is whether such offence is an offence relating to the business or operation of a bank so as to confer jurisdiction on the Tribunal.

Arguments advanced in favour of denying jurisdiction in the Gamji Bank case are that only the Attorney-General of a state can prosecute offences against state laws in state enactments43 and that the Federal Attorney-General has no power to do so. further, stealing under the Criminal Code is a general offence and not an offence "relating to the business or operation of a bank" even though the victim is a bank. It was also argued that the offence of stealing could not be an offence relating to banking since banking is on the exclusive legislative list over which a state government could not legislate44.

These arguments were not accepted by the Special Appeal Tribunal which held that

> the offence charged in this case are state offences. But the offences in our judgment do not relate to banks and banking but relate to the business or operation of a bank45."

and they could therefore be prosecuted by the Federal Attorney-General or a legal practitioner authorised by him.

The attraction of defence argument on this issue must be acknowledged. Carried to its logical conclusion Tribunals may be faced with trying offences of assault, defamation etc. committed in the course of banking business - a sphere which is not actually intended for them. However the procedural convenience of the appellate decision may be its justification.

8. Conclusion

The sanctions containea in the Decrees may rightly be described as a potent deterrent against banking malpractices. For high level management at least the prospect of imprisonment without option of a fine is not to be lightly regarded. Added to this is the traditional and justifiable fear of special tribunals and their tight procedures. But these without more cannot achieve the objectives of the Decree. Of paramount importance is diligence in the detection and prosecution of offences under the Decree. In the past prosecutions rarely occured because of cover-ups. This is why it is regrettable that the Decree does not deal specifically with failure to report or prosecute offences and to conceal or compound them. Banks appear unduly conscious of the possible adverse effects on their reputation of disclosure of large scale insider malpractices.

It is believed that the new legal framework will go a long way to sanitize the banking sector, make bank officials alive to the demands of good baking practices and ultimately restore full confidence in the banking industry.

Notes

1. There are presently about 47 distressed banks in the country: See "First Quarter Review of the Economy" by the Minister of Finance, Chief Anthony Ani, *Business Times*, Monday April 21, 1995, p. 5 at p. 29.
2. See *Business Times*, Monday April 24, 1995 p. 1. This report also shows that all categories of bank staff are involved in bank frauds, and that the number of bank staff disciplined for involvement in fraud rose from 313 in 1989 to 516 in 1993 - at p. 19. See "CBN Sounds Fraud Alarm to Banks," *The Guardian*, Sunday July 28, 1991 pp 1 and 2.
3. Cap. 301 L.F.N. 1990
4. Cap. 28 L.F.N. 1990 (repealed)
5. Cap. 59 L.F.N. 1990
6. S.1
7. S.3(1)
8. See Part II of the Decree
9. See s. 7 of the Criminal Code. See ss 21(4) and 23(4) of the Decree which are discussed below
10. See s. 515 of the Criminal Code
11. See s. 20(1)(a) of the Decree
12. See *Newswatch*, February 13, 1995 27, at p. 29
13. See ss. 98 and 116 C.C.
14. But see the definition of "director" in s.29. This includes the director's wife/husband, father, mother, son or daughter. The same does not apply to manager, officer or employee. In any event benefit conferred on a friend etc should be within the scope of this offence
15. See ss.98 and 116 C.C. See also s. 115 of the Penal Code.
16. S. 19(1)(e)
17. In Lagos State the conduct of an officer, who with knowledge of the borrower's ability to repay, grants a waiver, may amount to stealing. The borrower's indebtedness to the bank is a chose in action. Under the Lagos State Criminal Code (s.382), a thing in action is capable of being stolen. The fraudulent conversion of the chose in action is stealing

18. S. 19(3).
19. S. 21(2)
20. S. 21(3)
21. S. 21(4)
22. See also s. 22(2)
23. S. 20(1)(a)
24. See ss. 98 and 116 C.C.
25. S. 21(1)
26. The punishment prescribed in the Criminal Code for attempts is one-half of the punishments prescribed for the full offences. See ss. 509, 510 and 511 C.C.
27. See s. 512 C.C.
28. S. 22(1)
29. S. 16(2)
30. S. 16(2)
31. S. 20(2)
32. S. 20(3)
33. S. 20(4)
34. See *R* v. *Davies* [1965) Crim. L.R. 56; *R* v. *Whybrew* [1979] Crim. L.R. 599. *R* v. *wigley* [1978] Crim. L.R. 635
35. See D.A. Thomas, *Principles of Sentencing* (1st ed.) p. 197
36. See *President Ibadan Province* v. *Lagunju* (1954) 14 WACA 549
37. At p. 73 of the typed judgment
38. At pp. 71 - 73
39. Numbered (i), (ii), (iii), (v) and (vO) at pp. 71 - 73
40. At p. 36
41. At p. 37
42. See s. 383(2)(f)
43. In this case the Criminal Code of Lagos State
44. See the arguments of Chief F.R.A. Williams at pp. 16-17 citing *Queen* v. *Owoh* [1962] All N.L.R. (pt.2) 653, *Akwule* v. *The Queen* [1963] NRNLR. 105
45. At p. 18.

CHAPTER 4

Tribunals In Nigeria

By

Hon. Justice J.N.M. Onyechi
(Chairman Robbery and Fire-Arms Tribunal, Anambra State)

The Conception:

Tribunals in Nigeria have been subjected to criticism and castigations, some-times by some exponents of democracy and human rights outside and within Nigeria, including some legal practitioners on the Bench and at the Bar.

It could be easily ventured that Tribunals are sometimes not generally understood and conceived in proper perspectives.

Today's discourse on Tribunals in Nigeria will incidentally relate to our thoughts on Nigeria in the 21st Century, overviewing their reform and projection.

The Nigerian Constitutions from Independence till date made provisions for the fora that are expected at the various periods to dispense justice in the determination of the rights and obligations of Nigerians and nationals that would fall within the conspectus of law and justice of this Republic[2].

The fora reserved for the determination of the said rights and obligations or on occasions they arise for determination as a matter of primary issues or as necessary adjuncts in the circumstances, have always been in the language of the successive constitutional enactments

"The Court or other Tribunal."

This phrase beacons the forum envisaged in each Constitution and has to be interpreted legally.

Court and Tribunal are used here *sui generis* as birds of the same body. I dare say that they wear various feathers. Section 54 of the

Interpretation Act made provision for "or" "other" and "otherwise" to be construed disjunctively and not as applying similarity unless "similar" or some other word of like meaning is added. Therefore, because Tribunal is similar to Court and "other" prefixed it in the Constitutional provisions "Court or other Tribunal" means Court or other similar Court.

Here the layman would think differently if the word "Tribunal" is used instead of the word "Court." But the layman conceives the contents of "*Court*"" or "*Tribunal*" in these several constitutional entrenchments necessarily in their specific legal perspective.

Section 32 of the Constitution of the Federation of Nigeria, 1960 defined court in the chapter of the Constitution dealing with Fundamental Human Rights to mean -

"any court of law in Nigeria (other than a court - martial) and includes Her Majesty in Council: Provided that, in relation to a member of the armed forces of the crown, it includes a court - martial" [3]

This definition excluded express provisions or requirements relating to the word "*court.*" "The Armed Forces of the Crown" was changed into the Armed Forces of the Federal Republic of Nigeria after Nigeria became a Republic in 1963.

Also the final Court of the Republic which was Her Majesty-in-Council ordinarily called the Privy Council was replaced with the Supreme Court of the Federal Republic of Nigeria and this became the Highest Law Court of Appeal in the land. It was clothed with the acronym: the Highest Court of Law in the republic.

The question of whether Tribunals include the Law Courts or indeed the courts is implicit in the already stated phrase "*the Court or other Tribunals.*" This conception is based on the ordinary meaning attracted by the phrase as well as from the contexts in which they were used in the various enabling Acts, Decrees, Laws and Edicts in which they were provided. The enabling laws include the Constitutions of Nigeria previously referred to. The Concise Oxford Dictionary of the then Current English [4] gave the meaning of the word "Court" to be -

"Assembly of judges or other persons acting as Tribunal."

At page 1239 it defined *"Tribunal of Justice" as "Court of Justice."* The Stroud's Judicial Dictionary of Words and Phrases Judicially Interpreted and Statutory Definition[5] stated as follows:

"a Bishop's Commission of Inquiry under S.77, Pluralities Act, 1838 (1 & 2 Vict. C. 106) as amended by S. 348 & 49 Vict. C. 54; is a judicial Tribunal... It is clear from the foregoing expressions that a Court is a Tribunal and that a Court of Law is a Judicial Tribunal. Further, a Commission of Inquiry which deals with finding of facts and recommendations[6] is a Tribunal which could be a Judicial Tribunal or an Administrative Tribunal or Board or Commission of Inquiry.

This subject of Tribunals in Nigeria would therefore normally be administrative body, associations, institutional, judicial, religious, commercial and other functional regulatory and supervisory bodies which examine the rights and obligations of persons with respect to their acts and omissions in the course of their inquires into the act, conduct or omission of public officers under inquiry[7].

The emphases are on the fundamental rights and obligations of Nigerians and Persons. The acts and omissions may touch and concern the Republic or other Nigerians, animate or inanimate[8].

Section6(1) and (2) of the 1979 Constitution vested the Judicial powers of the Federation in the courts established for the Federation and the Courts established for each of the States of the Federation. These courts are the Superior Courts of Record or Courts given the powers of Superior Courts of Record[9]. The Courts established by the Constitution as Superior Courts of Record are by virtue of Section6(3) of the Constitution (*ibid*) the following:

(1) The Supreme Court of Nigeria;
(2) The Court of Appeal;
(3) The Federal High Courts,
(4) The High Courts of the States of the Federation;
(5) The Sharia Courts of Appeal of the States that needed them; and
(6) The Customary Courts of Appeal of the States that needed them.

The Courts to be established by any State of the Federation and donated with the powers of a Superior Court of Record in their enabling Statutes are as follows:

(1) Courts authorised to exercise the power of a Superior Court of Record by the National Assembly in the enabling Federal Statute;
(2) Courts authorised to exercise the power of a Superior Court of Record in the enabling State Statute by the State Assembly at first instance or on appeals.

The proposition is that at the Federal level the other Tribunals established to exercise the powers of a Superior Court of Record are the following:

(1) The Miscellaneous Offences Tribunals set up under the Special Tribunals (Miscellaneous Offences) Decree, 1984.
(2) The Tribunals for Trial of Offences established as the various Miscellaneous Offences Tribunals in Zones.
(3) The Counterfeit Currency Tribunal set up by virtue of the Counterfeit Currency (Special Provisions) Decree, 1984.
(4) The Exchange Control Anti-Sabotage Tribunal set up by virtue of the Exchange Control (Anti-Sabotage) Decree, 1984.
(5) The Federal Banks Recovery of Debts and Financial Malpractices constituted by virtue of the failed Banks (Recovery of Debts) and Financial Malpractices in Banks Decree 1994.
(6) The Failed Contracts Recovery of Debts and Financial Malpractices Tribunal now mooted to be established by the Federal Military Government.
(7) The Civil Disturbances Tribunals established under the Civil Disturbances (Special Tribunal) Act (Cap 53 Laws of the Federation of Nigeria) 1990.
(8) Tribunals for the Trial of Students Delinquency like belonging to secret Society or Examinations Malpractices.
(9) Other Tribunals set up under the Commissions of Inquiry Act of the Republic or regarding Section 33(2) of the 1979 Constitution or Section 35(2) of the proposed 1989 Constitution

to determine questions arising in the administration of a Decree or Act or other law that affects or may affect the civil rights and obligations of persons.

Another suggestion is that at State level the other Tribunals established to exercise the powers of a Superior Court of Record are the following:

(1) The Robbery and Firearms Tribunals established vide the Robbery and Firearms (Special Provisions) Decree, 1984.
(2) The Tribunal on the Recovery of Public Funds and Property set up under the Recovery of Public Property (Special Military Tribunals) Decree 1984.
(3) Other Tribunals or Commissions of Inquiry established under the Commission of Inquiry Law of the States, as the case may be, and regarding Section 33(2) of the 1979 Constitution or 35(2) of the 1983 Constitution to determine questions arising in the administration of a law that affects or may affect the civil rights and obligations of any person.

All these Tribunals are mainly established under the Federal Decrees or Acts. In respect of both the above first categories the Federal Government funds them and the second category which, the enabling Decree or Act empowers the State Government to establish, are funded by State Government. These later Tribunals include the Robbery and Firearms Tribunals in the States of the Federation and Tribunals under the Recovery of Public Property (Special Military Tribunals) Decree 1984.

The Chairman And Members of Tribunals

There is a difference between the establishment of the ordinary courts on the one hand and the other Tribunals on the other hand. The difference is that unlike Judges of the Ordinary Courts, the other Tribunal's Chairman is appointed by the Government either of the Federation or of the State.

The Hon. State Chief Judge usually recommends a retired or serving Judge for appointment by the Government or the Administrator of a State as Chairman of the Tribunal. In the case of other Federal Tribunals the Hon. Chief Justice of Nigeria or the Federal Attorney-General and Minister of Justice recommends the incumbent Chairman.

The other memberships are recommended by the Federal Attorney-General and Minister of Justice on the nomination of the Authority like the Branch of the Armed Forces of the Republic, for appointment by the Federal Government in the case of a Federal Tribunal. In the case of the State Tribunal, the nominating authority is the same but the appointment shall be by the Civil or Military Governor or Administrator of the State. The Attorney-General and Commissioner for Justice or the Secretary to the Military or Civilian Government recommends the Civilian Members who are sometimes Legal Practitioners, presented at times by the Attorney-General of the state.

The Federal Tribunal Chairman and Members are sworn by the Hon. Chief Justice of Nigeria. But the performance oath or oath of office the Chairman and Members of a State Tribunal are made before the Military or Civilian Governor or Administrator of the State concerned.

The Chairman of the Tribunals is either a Serving or Retired Judicial Officer of any of the Superior Courts of Record in Nigeria[10]. Most enabling Laws specify that he shall be a Serving or Retired Judge of the Federal or State High Court or of the High Court of the Federal Capital Territory of Abuja. The membership are either members of the Army and the Police. Generally they are enacted to be serving members of the Armed Forces. Reference here is to the Army, Air Force and the Navy. Where they remain members, they should not be below the rank of a Major of the Armed Forces or its equivalent. For a Police Officer he should not be below the rank of a Chief Superintendent of Police.

The Civilian Members are mostly Legal Practitioners. In the case of the Civil Disturbances Tribunal, former Ambassadors and retired Commissioners of Police or top Police Officers were appointed.

The Non-Judicial Members including the Military and Police Officers are no longer members of the various Tribunals established under the following Decrees[11]:

(1) The Recovery of Public Property (Special Military Tribunals) Decree 1984;
(2) The Exchange Control (Anti-Sabotage) Decree 1984;
(3) The Special Tribunal (Miscellaneous Offences) Decree 1984;
(4) The Counterfeit Currency (Special Provisions) Decree 1984; and
(5) The Transition to Civil Rule (Political Programme) Decree 1987.

This withdrawal of the Non-Judicial Members affected Military and Police Officers in the main. It did not extend to all the Tribunals established under other Decrees or Laws of the Republic or of the States[12].

However, it gave a retired or serving Judge specified power to sit alone in the Tribunals in trying a part-heard case *de novo* except where it is not possible to do so for one reason or the other subject to the powers of the Attorney-General of the Federation in respect of prosecuting offenders under Section 160(1)(c) of the Constitution of the federal Republic of Nigeria 1979 as amended [13].

A Tribunal also exercises exclusive jurisdiction over all ancillary matters, including remand, bail and any other preliminary issues connected with an offence over which the Tribunal has jurisdiction. This was specifically enacted for the Tribunals established under the Recovery of Public Property (Special Military Tribunals) Decree 1984, Exchange Control (Anti-Sabotage) Decree 1984, Special Tribunals (Miscellaneous Offences) Decree 1984, Counterfeit Currency (Special Provisions) Decree 1984, Transition to Civil Rule (Political Programme) Decree 1987.

However, the application of either the Criminal Procedure Code, Criminal Procedure Law or Act, as the case may be, supervenes in dealing with the trial of the tribunal Offences and imports powers dealing with contemnors to the Tribunal, the Chairman, Members of the tribunal and the Tribunal proceedings including its judgment in the circumstances.

The Provision For Tribunal Effectiveness And Independence

In order to ensure the effectiveness and independence of these Tribunals, it was enacted by the Tribunals (Miscellaneous Provisions) Decree 1991[14] as follows:

(1) The Supervisory jurisdiction or power of judicial review of the High Court shall not extend to any matter or proceedings before a Tribunal which was duly constituted before or after 16th January 1991 when the decree came into effect.

(2) Any proceedings brought before any High Court relating to the supervisory jurisdiction or power of judicial review of a High Court on a cause or matter brought before a Tribunal after the commencement of this Decree, shall abate, cease or be deemed to be discontinued without any further assurance other than this Decree.

Also reserved is the fairness provisions as follows:

(1) No person, who has taken part in the search for, pursuit or apprehension of any person to be tried or who has taken part in the investigation of any person to be tried, shall act as a member of the Tribunal constituted for the trial of that person in respect of any of the Tribunal Offences[15].

(2) No civil proceedings shall lie or be instituted in any court for or on account of or in respect of any act, matter or thing done or purported to be done under or pursuant to the Decree creating the Tribunal and if any such proceedings are instituted before, on or after the commencement of the said Decree, the proceedings shall abate, be discharged and made void[16].

(3) There is also the offence of contempt of the Tribunal which exists for the protection of the authority, honour and integrity of the Tribunal, the Chairman and the Members. This offence arises in areas of failure of an offender or witness to answer to the demands of a summons or warrant to appear to testify at the hearing or, in the case of a person on bail, for trial or continued trial or for judgment in his case. This applies where there is lacuna in providing the procedure for the trial of a Tribunal Offences[17].

The Tribunal Trial As Adversary

The adversary system of criminal procedure of upholding the innocence of the offender until the prosecution proves him guilty of the offence charged beyond reasonable doubt is paramount. In this regard, when an offender makes no plea to a charge on the information before a Tribunal or he refuses to plead, this is recorded and the Tribunal is obliged to treat the situation as a plea of not guilty and make an entry of a plea of not guilty where the offence charged is punishable with death[18]. On the occasion when the offender pleads not guilty, the Tribunal shall enter the plea of not guilty and proceed, either on that day of plea or on subsequent hearing day or days, to try the case. In trying the case, the prosecutor shall examine the witnesses for the prosecution one after the other and each witness shall in turn be cross-examined by the accused or his counsel. The prosecutor shall thereafter re-examine the witnesses after their respective cross-examination.

Where the offender pleads not guilty or makes no plea or refuses to plead or if the Tribunal enters a plea of not guilty on behalf of the offender, the law is that the offender put his case before the Tribunal for determination of his guilt or innocence. The Tribunal shall therefore proceed to try the case[19].

At the end of this course of procedure, the Tribunal shall ask the accused through his Defence Counsel, if he has one, as follows:

(a) Whether he wishes to testify on his own behalf;
(b) Whether he intends to call witnesses other than witnesses as to his character.

If the accused person or his counsel desires any of these two alternatives-

(1) He would be asked to present his witnesses who shall be led by him or his Counsel, be then cross-examined by the prosecutor and re-examined by his Counsel or himself.

(2) In the event of the accused or his Counsel choosing to call witnesses other than witness as to his character on his behalf, his witness would testify-in-chief, be cross-examined by the prosecutor or his Counsel as was the case with the prosecution witnesses. In respect

of the first alternative of not wishing to testify or call witness other than of his character, the prosecuting Counsel may sum up his case against the accused before the accused or his counsel may reply. At that stage, the Tribunal may, on considering that no case has been made out for the accused person to defend, enter that the accused has no case to answer on the charge and discharge him[20]. The prosecution or his Counsel, may sum up his case against the offender before presenting his evidence. He may also sum up his case against any one or more of the offender against whom he consider the evidence not sufficient to justify continuing the trial against the said offender or offenders.

The Tribunal may, however, at the will of the accused person or his Counsel or in its discretion and after considering the evidence presented by the prosecutor, take his evidence and or that of his witnesses, after the prosecution has opened his case stating the facts or law which he intends to rely on. The prosecution shall then lead his witnesses in evidence in chief one by one and the offender or his Counsel shall cross-examine them before their re-examination by the prosecution or his Counsel. Thereafter the Tribunal shall consider the evidence and the law in respect of the case after hearing the address by the prosecution or his Counsel and then the offender or his Counsel. The Tribunal shall record its decision and pronounce same. Such decision would be either that the prosecution has proved its case against the accused person or that the prosecution has failed to prove the case against the accused. Such proof shall be beyond reasonable doubt upon giving effect to any of the two alternative findings. Then the Tribunal would acquit and discharge the offender person if he is not found guilty. On the other hand, if the offender is found guilty, the Tribunal would receive evidence as to his character or facts in mitigation. After the Tribunal has considered the circumstances and facts following the plea *ad misercordiam* by him and his Counsel, the Tribunal shall then make any of the following sentence or order:-

(1) The verdict of caution and discharge where it is not statutorily disallowed;

(2) Pronounce a verdict of binding over against the future conduct of the offender where this is possible;

(3) Sentence the offender to terms of imprisonment as stipulated by the enabling Decree;

(4) Sentence the offender to death by firing squad or by hanging as the case may be.

The prosecution is entitled to reply where the offender calls any witness other than as to his character. But where he calls such evidence as to his character the prosecution has right to adduce evidence of the offenders previous conviction. The prosecution may also reply on a point of law or any new matter or evidence. Thereafter the Tribunal may rise or adjourn.

When the conviction and sentences of the Tribunal are made, the Tribunal shall then enter the court and announce its findings. When he is found guilty the conviction and sentence are subject to the confirmation or refusal of the Governor or Administrator of the State. If confirmed, the procedure for carrying out the sentence, whether reduced or allowed to stand, will proceed. This is not an inquisitorial procedure in the circumstances of the above exposition on the procedure provided on the enabling Decrees.

The trial procedure is adversary and prevails in all the Judicial Tribunals of the Land[21].

The Article (*ibid)* provided the right of offenders to defend and be defended by Counsel of the offender's choice. These rights are provided for in Section (3) of the Civil Disturbances (Special Tribunal) Act, which reserved for the defence of the offender by only a legal practitioner who is resident in Nigeria. These rights were enshrined in Section 33(c) of the 1979 Constitution.

The enactment in Rule 5 on the Schedule to the Robbery and Firearms (Special Provisions) Decree 1984 provided *inter alia:*

> where an accused charged with an offence punishable with death is not defended by a legal practitioner, the tribunal shall assign a legal practitioner for his defence.

This enjoins the Tribunal to assign a legal practitioner for the defence of only an offender who is charged with an offence punishable with death where he has none[22].

Such a person facing the capital offence could, therefore, not be tried until this course has been employed. The Counsel would then conduct his defence by cross-examining the prosecution witnesses and, if need be, leading the accused person and or his witnesses in their testimony in his defence. He could raise any preliminary issues arising in the proceedings or on the charge. He could also make a no case submission at the close of the prosecution's case or address the Tribunal on behalf of the accused person at the end of the evidence of the prosecution and or that of the defence, as the case may be.

This hearing procedure of the Tribunals is no doubt in line with the procedure of the ordinary Law Courts of the Republic. The adversary system of criminal trial requires that the facts alleged by the prosecution in charging the offender must be proved in order to rebut the presumption of the innocence of the offender. If it were not so, the practice becomes the system where-upon the offender being charged and arraigned for an offence, it would be the onus on the part of the offender to establish that he is not guilty of the offence with which he is charged or such offence or offences arising from the facts against him and which arises or arise upon the offence or offences charged against him. In this particular circumstance, the trial would be by reason or inquisitorial system.

This inquisitorial system enjoins that generally an offender charged with an offence shall not be presumed to be innocent until he proves the contrary. It is such proof of innocence by the offender that both our Constitutions at least since Independence and later Article 7(b) of the African Charter on Human and People's Rights (Ratification and Enforcement) Act 1983 enshrined for the benefit of an offender.

The inquisitorial practice was prevalent in the continent of Europe whose criminal trial followed the Roman Law System and was their dominant law as opposed to the common law which the adversary system epitomises.

It is worthy of note that even the customary law requires that an allegation must be proved, and, like the common law, presumption relative to such proof, arises from the testimony of witnesses. The standard of proof may differ from the requirements of the adversary system according to the infraction but generally it could be the same.

It is the allegations for which the witnesses are called that gave rise to the offender being brought forward before-

(1) The Elders of his family in the first instance;
(2) The Elders of the village in the second instance;
(3) The Elders of the town presided over by the traditional ruler of the town assisted by his *ndichie* in the final instance.

This cannot be an inquisitorial procedure as it is often alluded to or conceived in modern circles. It should not be forgotten that, unless accepted by any party complying with the decision at customary law or by written acceptance, the aggrieved party could fly to the law courts usually the High Court, Magistrate Court or the Customary or Area Court, as the case may be, for re-hearing.

It is note-worthy that there exist preliminary procedures which precede arraignment, trial and discharge or conviction and sentence. This preliminary procedure takes place whether the trial is adversary and even in inquisitorial systems of trial. It is this preliminary practice that breeds the conception that the inquisitorial system obliterates the need for the presumption of innocence of an offender being tried under it. But signatories to the United Nations covenant on civil and political rights and the African Charter on Himan and Peoples Rights are from the common law and the Codified System of the inquisitorial systems. The practice blends the Police investigation and the vetting of the case file with the statements of witnesses prevalent in the adversary system at its preliminary stage.

It is after this preliminary step is employed, to enable investigation to be conducted as to whether the conduct or negligence or otherwise of persons arrested for the special offences triable before a Tribunal requires trial at the Tribunal if it is satisfied that any person prima facie committed an offence triable by the Tribunal[23]. The offences could be modified at Section 1(1)(2) and (3) of the Civil Disturbances (Special Tribunal) Act 1987, by the President and Commander-in-Chief of the Armed Forces of Nigeria. The Members of this Special Committee were also appointed by the President and Commander-in-Chief of the Armed Forces of the Republic and he has the power to grant them general or specific directions. They however have power to regulate their own proceedings as they may deem fit.

The Preliminary procedures of Scotland and France reputedly said to originate from the Code System characterised by its Roman

Law origin and the Inquisitorial System, is in the form of pre-trial inquiries. This was explained inter alia:

> there are three types of pre-trial inquiries -
>
> 'l'enquete flagrante,'
>
> 'l'enquete preliminaire'
>
> (both of which are conducted by the Police and the procureur de la Republique) and 'l' information judiciaire' (which is conducted by a Judge d' instruction)[24].

These were elaborated as follows:-

(1) Specific action with regard to post-mortem examinations, search and seizure, arrest and detention ("garde a rue"), termination of detention, and procureur's questioning the accused and to end the powers of the procureur. The prosecution of the proceedings with his discretion to order no further proceedings in the matter.

(2) The specific actions of l'enquete preliminaire to arrest and detain an alleged offender with power of the procureur to order no further proceedings, depending on the facts presented to him against the offender.

(3) The *achous* in aid of the information judiciaire for a Judge d'instruction for the instruction judiciare are instigation of inquiries, the types of offences that may be instigated, secrecy of inquiries vis-a-vis the Press, the dossier, the duties and powers of a judge d' instruction, warrants of arrest, pre-trial custody. examination of the witnesses, confrontations relative to reconstructions, use of experts, search and seizure, background inquiries on resultant dossier du'personnalite, termination of inquiries by the Judge d'instruction and the rights of parties and relationship to the Judge d'instruction. This is followed by Chambere d'accusation during which there could be committal for trial, extradiction and exercise of the powers of the President.

These precede the judicial proceedings of the Court Trial at which the innocence or guilt of the accused is determined before the tribunal order and or sentence is entered on the record of the Court and pronounced by the Judge or Court.

These pre-trial procedures follow the common law processes of the Investigation Committee as follows:-

(1) In order to determine whether to charge for trial persons or group of persons for their conduct, negligence or otherwise which, howsoever, caused in any way or contributed to the outbreak of civil disturbances, in the light of its findings on the facts brought before it

(2) Whether any person or group of persons propagating or holding religious, political, social or any movement or association howsoever called led by any person or group of persons contributed to or participated in any way in the civil disturbances;

(3) Whether any person or persons being citizens of Nigeria or not, encouraged, contributed to or participated in the civil disturbances[25].

This Special Investigation Committee is constituted by the President and Commander-in-Chief of the Armed Forces of the Republic where he shares the opinion as follows:

(1) There has occured civil disturbances, commotions or unrest in any part of the Federal Republic of Nigeria;

(2) There has been a breach of the peace and tranquility of the nation;

(3) The public order and public safety of Nigeria is being threatened by any disturbance;

(4) There has occured or may likely occur a riot or civil disturbances of a riotous nature resulting or likely to result, as the case may be, in loss of life and property or injury to person[26].

Investigations follow Police action in respect of offences which are not classified as special offences for trial at the Tribunals under exposition in this lecture. This covers up to the arraignment at the Magistrates Court for remand or discharge of offences. They also embrace the preliminary investigations of old at the Magistrates Courts and the present procedure for taking and considering the proof of evidence at the Department of the Public Prosecutions of the Ministry of Justice to enable the Hon. Attorney-General or persons acting on his behalf to initiate and prosecute the offender for alleged discovered Tribunal offences[27].

Criminal trials before the Tribunals are for offences under the following:

(1) Section 3(2) of the Special Tribunals (Miscellaneous Offences) Decree 1984. These are triable at the Special Miscellaneous Offences Tribunal of the various Zones of Nigeria and the punishments are stated at Section 6 of the Decree of 1984 (*ibid*).

(2) Section 1 to 4 of the Robbery and Firearms (Special Provisions) Decree 1984, including Sections 3A, 4 and 4A of the Robbery and Firearms (Special Provisions) (Amendment) Decree 1986. The punishments are included therein

(3) The offences at the First Schedule as A - Criminal Code and B - Penal Code, for trial at the Civil Disturbances Special Tribunal.

The offences are extensions of those listed on the Criminal Code of the Federation as well as the Criminal Codes of the States of the Federal Republic. The sentences were no doubt varied upwards to be in line with the seriousness and promptness attached to dealing with them as economic or stability offences.

The Quorum of the Special Tribunals are as follows:

(1) The Chairman and any three other members of the Civil Disturbances Special Tribunal: Section 2(3) of the Civil Disturbances (Special Tribunal) Act 1987.

(2) The Special Miscellaneous Offences Tribunal has the Judge constituting the Tribunal who can sit alone after the other members except the Chairman were decreed not to be in the membership of the tribunal any more by Section 1 of the Tribunals (Miscellaneous Provisions) Decree 1991, by providing a new Sub-Section (12)(3)(5)(6) thereof.

(3) The Robbery and Firearms (Special Provisions) Decree No.5 of 1984 as amended by Section 5 of its amendment Decree 1986 which stipulated that a Judge, that is the Chairman, can sit alone.

The proceeding provision of the new Section 27 of the interpretation Act or Decree introduced by Section 2(1) of the said Interpretation (Amendment) Decree No. 44 of 1987 is that the quorum of any Tribunal, Commission or Inquiry shall be the

Chairman and a member, who were present at every sitting of the Tribunal throughout the duration of the trial or hearing of the Tribunal, including any appeal arising from the decision or judgement of the Tribunal, Commission or Inquiry before the Appeal Tribunal established for the purpose.

There are extensions of the offences to be tried by Special Miscellaneous Tribunals constituted mainly as a result of the clamour of Nigerians beleaguered by social and economic crimes because they itch for quick decisive action to control or stop them. Their intendment is the promotion of peace and quiet for reasonable development. The Tribunals were therefore instruments thus conceived for the security and stability of the nation. These Tribunals are the Special Miscellaneous Offences Tribunals constituted under the Special Tribunals (Miscellaneous Offences) Decree 1984 as amended to try offences, being elaborations of offences under the Criminal Code of the Republic or of the States by the Principal Decree 1984. This was amended by replacing them with other elaborated offences, *vide* the Special Tribunals (Miscellaneous Offences) (Amendment) Decree No.21 of 1986 and No.22 of 1986.

Other Special Miscellaneous Offences Tribunals were established and the Offences relating to them which were contained in the Special Tribunals (Miscelaneous Offences) Decrees No.20 of 1984, No.21 of 1986 and No.22 of 1986, were either extended further or replaced variously by the said Decrees. This was mainly in 1995. The Decrees were as follows:

(1) Money Laundering Decree No.3 of 1995

(2) Advance Fee Fraud and Other Fraud Related Offences decree No. 13 of 1995

(3) Failed Banks (Recovery of Debts) and Financial Malpractices in Banks Decree No.18 of 1994 as amended by the Amendment Decree No.18 of 1995.

(4) Telecommunications and Postal Offences Decree No.21 of 1995.

The Recovery of Public Property (Special Military Tribunals) Decree No. 3 of 1984 stands alone as one of the steps taken in 1984 to instill consciousness for discipline, order and security in Nigeria immediately after the December 1993 Military Coup. This was quickly amended by the Amendment Decree No.14 of 1984. It made provisions for a Military Tribunal ordinarily referred to as Panel but it was headed by a serving or retired High Court Judge with three Military Officers not below the rank of a Leutenant Colonel or its equivalent[29] as members.

Some Tribunals were generally required to institute, try and transmit records of the proceedings of the tribunal offence within a specified time or period. This appears to be in line with the 1979 Constitution of Nigeria. In the case of the Armed Robbery and Firearms (Special Provisions) Decree 1984, as amended, the provision is as follows:

(1) The proceedings shall be instituted within 7 days from the receipt at the Ministry of Justice of the Police case file containing the completed Police investigation in respect of a capital offence for which the offender was apprehended under Section 1(2) of the Decree of 1984, as amended.

(2) The trial shall be concluded within 7 days of the Tribunal's first trial in respect of the offence.

(3) The Registrar of the Tribunal shall, not later than 7 days after the conclusion and conviction of the said offender, forward a copy of the record of proceedings to office of the appropriate Military Governor or Administrator.

The main purpose is for the Military Governor or Administrator to consider and confirm or disallow any conviction or sentence imposed by the Tribunal after convicting and sentencing the offender -

(a) Not later than 7 days in the case of a person convicted of a capital offence.

(b) Not later than 30 days in respect of an offender convicted and sentenced for other offences under the Decree No.5 of 1984.

Implicit here is that all offenders can petition to the Military Administrator or Governor to review their conviction and or sentence on grounds for which he could have appealed if there was an Appeal Court.

The Military Administrator or Governor would seek the advice of the Attorney-General and Commissioner for Justice of his State before acting on the record of proceedings transmitted to him by the Registrar of the Tribunal. A similar reference is made where the convicted and sentenced offender petitioned him for review of his position. Here a copy of the proceedings would have been given to him or his Counsel in any case. Because of these, three (3) copies of the proceedings are usually sent to the Military Governor or Administrator so that he can keep one and transmit two to the Hon Attorney-General and Commissioner for Justice. Usually the Attorney-General refers the case to his Law Officer, usually the Director of Public Prosecutions for advice. He, in turn, would refer the case for review or for the Governor's or Administrator's confirmation or refusal of the conviction and sentence, to a State Counsel for advice.

Future Projection

There is no provision for appeal in respect of the Robbery and Firearms Tribunal decisions. The new Section 27 of the Interpretation Act, as amended, suggests that there is appeal against decisions or recommendations of a Tribunal, Commission or Inquiry. But Section 13(2) of the Recovery of Public Property (Special Military Tribunals)(Amendment) Decree No.21 of 1986 and Section 1 of the Recovery of Public Property (Special Military Tribunals) Amendment Decree No.22 of 1987 provided for Special Appeal Tribunal to handle appeals from the Tribunal with the Appeal Judges constituted from among serving or retired Court of Appeal Justices. The Advance Fee Fraud and other Fraud Related Offences decree (*ibid*) provided for appeal to this Special Appeal Tribunal at Section 15(1) for final decision as provided at subsection(2) thereof.

These provisions for review by petition, or, by way of appeal, is intended to achieve the same result. But the course is different. The main trials are conducted in the full glare of the public. Sometimes these are televised by the television crew or reported by mass media reporters present at the Tribunal during its proceedings at the trial. The appeal where it exists is done by the offender or his Counsel on the one hand and the State respondent through Law Officers or State

Counsel, all in open Tribunal like in ordinary run of cases on appeal. This has its merits.

It is to be recalled that the Hon Attorney-General or the Solicitor-General by himself or through the law officers or State Counsel on his behalf, initiate proceedings for trial in the Tribunals. He also acts on the order of the Tribunal.

The question is why should he advise action by the Military Governor or Administrator regarding his confirmation or rejection or revision of the Tribunals conviction and sentence.

The Human Rights activists inside and outside Nigeria project criticisms of Tribunals. They adhere to adversary procedure of trial of offenders before it. They also observe the requirements of the rule of law and human rights provisions.

The question remains whether the appointment and composition of those Tribunals which still share Military, Public or Civilian membership, do so in keeping with the Constitution of the Republic, the African Charter on Human and Peoples Rights (Ratification and Enforcement) Act Cap 10, Laws of the Federal Republic of Nigeria 1990 and the United Nations Covenant on Civil and Political Rights relative to Courts or Tribunals and their procedures.

There are other areas open for reform for the 21st Century Nigeria. This reform is to make it abundantly vivid that all *sinues* for justice dispensation exist among the Tribunals.

The objection often taken is on the composition of these Tribunals especially regarding the presence of the Army or Police personnel on it.

The argument is that because justice must not only be done but must be seen as done and that people present or who heard the judgment see that fairness prevailed. In every particular case heard by the Tribunals, the same standard for measuring the independence of the courts should apply to the other Tribunals.

Experience, particularly of the writer, is that the membership of the Military or the Police has not impugned the Tribunal's independence, fairness and justice and that there has not been interference by the Government, the Military or the Police for favour or bias in the course or conclusions of the Tribunals' cases or actions in respect thereof.

Be that as it may, the fear that it could happen leads to the issue of the advisability of retaining Police and Military presence in any of these Tribunals. This was the feature which was set to be expunged from certain Tribunals by the Tribunals (Miscellaneous Provisions) Decree (Decree No.9 of 1991). This it did at Section 1 of the Decree when it stipulated *inter alia:*

> the enactments specified in column one of Schedule 1 to this Decree are hereby amended as follows, that is-
>
> by deleting subsection (2) of each enactment in column two and substituting therefore the following new provisions, that is - 6(2) A tribunal shall consist of a retired Judge of the Federal High Court or the High Court of a State or of the Federal Capital Territory, Abuja.

It went on to supplant sub-section (2) of the Tribunals (Miscellaneous Provisions) Decree 1991 with the following replacement enactments -

> all Criminal causes or matters before a Tribunal and every proceeding subsequent thereto shall be heard and disposed of by a single Judge as prescribed in subsection (2) of this section.

We are here not dealing with all Tribunals in the country.

We have not expatiated on Commissions or Tribunals of Inquiry. This would have been the topic for its own paper.

Suffice it that there is generally no interference or deliberate bias in the Judicial Tribunals discussed in this paper.

Suffice it to say that Tribunals should be constituted by a single Judge and in the case of membership only serving or retired Judges of the High Courts of the realm should qualify. In the case of Special Appeal Tribunals, the Justices of the Court of Appeal should qualify but that in the case of its Chairman he should be a retired Justice of the Supreme Court or a retired President of the Court of Appeal.

These Tribunals and the Special Appeal Tribunal should continue to be a feature of the Courts or other Tribunals of the Republic. And this ought to be so even up to 21st Century whether the Government is Military or Civilian.

Conclusion

We have explored Judicial Tribunals as other Tribunals related to the law courts. We treated their conceptions, protections and procedures. We entered the dream-land regarding its future in the 21st century.

Notes

2. See the constitution of the Federation of Nigeria, 1960, Section 21(1) and proviso to Sub-Section(3); the Constitution of the federation of Nigeria, 1963, Section 22(1) and proviso to Sub-Section (3) thereof the Constitution of the Federal Republic of Nigeria, 1979, Section 33(1) and (3) and proviso to Sub-Section (4) thereof and the Constitution of the Federal Republic of Nigeria, 1989, Section 35(1), (3) and proviso to Sub-Section (12) thereof.

3. See, also, Section 33 of the 1963 Constitution which defined 'Court' to mean any court of law in Nigeria, but except in relation to a member of the armed forces of the Federation does not include court-martial as in effect the quoted S.32 of the 1963 Constitution above.

4. See page 235 of the 3rd Impression 1976 of the 6th Edition of the Dictionary.

5. See page 956 of the 1931 Edition of the Dictionary. The Act referred to was enacted during the reign of Queen Victoria of Great Britain and was set in Chapters referred as "C". While Her Majesty's Statutes were simply abbreviated to read (1 & 2 Vict. C. 106) or (S.348 & 49 Vict. C. 54).

6. See, for instance Section 2(1) 7, 19 the Commissions of Inquiry Law Cap 23 Vol.11 and 21 of Laws of the Western Region of Nigeria 1959. This has been adapted and made for the various Western States. There are similar Laws for the other States of Nigeria. The Federation has its own Commissions of Inquiry Act for the Republic for similar objective.

7. Particular reference is also made to Sections 17(1), 20(1)(a) to (c), 21(1) to (3), (5)(d) and proviso to S. 21(5)(8) and proviso to Sub-Section (1) and Sub-Section 29 and 31(3) of the 1960 Constitution. Also 18(1), 27(2)(b), proviso to Sub-Section(1), Sub-Section(2), S.31(b), S.32 of the 1963 Constitution; 30(1), 32(1)(a) to (c), 33(1)(3)(4)(6)(d)(7) and (9), S.40(b) and (e) and S.42(1) to (4)(a)of the 1979 Constitution.

8.See Section 6(5)(a) to (f) of the Constitution of the Federal Republic of Nigeria 1979 or of the 1989 Constitution which has not taken effect.

9. See Section (6)(g) and (h) of the 1979 Constitution. See also Section 6(b)(g) and (h) of the 1989 Constitution (*ibid*).

10. See, Section 2(2)(a) of the Civil Disturbances (Special Tribunal) Act (*ibid*)

11. See, Tribunals (Miscellaneous Provisions) Decree 1991, particularly Section 1 and also Sub-Section (6) thereof.

12. See, Section 2 of the Tribunals (Miscellaneous Provisions) Decree 1991 read together with the Schedule 1 thereof with reference to Section 2 (2)(a) and (b) and (11)(b) of the Special Tribunals (Miscellaneous Offences) Decree 1984.

13. See, Section 2(4) of the Special Tribunals (Miscellaneous Offences) Decree 1984 as introduced by Section 1 of the Tribunals (Miscellaneous Provisions) Decree 1991 as it relates also to Section 2(2)(a) and (b) of the Civil Disturbances (Special Tribunal) Act 1987. Also relative provisions of the Recovery of Public Property (Special Military Tribunals) Decree 1984.

14. See Sub-Sections (8) and (9) of Section 1 of the said Decree.

15. See the proviso to Section(2) of the Robbery and Firearms (Special Provisions) Decree 1984, proviso to Sub-Section (3) of Section 2 of the Civil Disturbances (Special Tribunal) Act (*ibid*) and Section 2(3) of the Special Tribunal (Miscellaneous Offences) Decree 1984.

16. Section 8(1) of the Special Tribunal (Miscellaneous Offences) Decree 1984

17. See Rule 16 of the procedure on the Schedule to the Special Tribunals (Miscellaneous Offences) Decree 1984 which allows the application of Criminal Procedure Act with modifications as circumstances may require, in trying Tribunal Offences which should be done in the same way as in the trial of Offences generally.

Also Section 3(4) of the Civil Disturbances (Special Tribunal) Act (*ibid)* and Rule 17 on the 2nd Schedule thereto; and Rule 18 of the Schedule to the Robbery and Firearms (Special Provisions) Decree 1984 which requires that the Provisions of the Criminal Procedure Code or depending on the venue, the Criminal Procedure Act shall apply with necessary modifications.

18. See Rule 3(2) of the Schedule to the Robbery and Firearms (Special Provisions) Decree 1984. See also Rule 3(2) of the Second Schedule to the Civil Disturbances (Special Tribunal Act 1987 which extended the provision to offences punishable with imprisonment for life.

19. The total consequences are provided in Rule 4 of Schedule to the Robbery and Firearms (Special Provisions) Decree 1984 and Rule 4 of Second Schedule to the Civil Disturbances (Special Tribunal) Act 1987 for instance.

20. See Rules 3 to 13 of the Schedule to the Decree No. 5 of 1984. Also Rules (3) to (10) of the Civil Disturbances (Special Tribunal) Act and Rules (3) to (10) on the Schedule to the Special Tribunal (Miscellaneous) (Miscellaneous Offences) Decree 1984. Also in respect of conforming reducing or refusing any sentence see Section 8(a)(b) and (c) and 9 of the Amended Decree No.5 of 1984 and Section 7(1)(2)(3)and (4) of the Civil Disturbances (Special Provisions) Act 1987 for instance.

21. See also Section 35(5)(c) of the 1989 Constitution.

22. See Section 4(3) of the Civil Disturbances (Special Tribunal) Act 1987 and Rule 5 at the Schedule to the Robbery and Firearms (Special Provisions) Decree 1984.

23. See Rule 2 of the Second Schedule to the Civil Disturbances (Special Tribunal) Act 1987, Rule 2 of the Schedule to the Robbery and Firearms (Special Provisions) Decree 1984 and Rule 2 of the Schedule to the Special Tribunal (Miscellaneous Offences) Decree 1984.

24. Schean, A.V., *Criminal Procedure in Scotland and France* (Scotland: N.P.) P.34.

25. See section 1(2) of the Civil Disturbances (Special Tribunal) Act 1987.

26. See Section 1(1) of the Civil Disturbances (Special Tribunal) Act 1987. Example is Zango-Kataf and Tafawa Balewa Local Government where trials later took place. Also the Kafanchan riots and the Civil Disturbances at Onitsha including the alleged OMATA self help, the disturbances in 1979 at Onitsha etc.

27. See Sections 3 to 35 of the Criminal Procedure Act *et Seg.* Section 5 of the Special Tribunal (Miscellaneous Offences) Decree 1984.

28. See Section 2(2)(a) and (b) of the Amendment Decree No.21 of 1986

CHAPTER 5

The Applicability Of Some "Inconsistent" Defences In The Nigerian Criminal Code

By

Frank I. Asogwah Esq.
LL.B (Hons) B.L., LL.M (Nig)
Lecturer; Faculty of Law
University of Nigeria, Enugu Campus

Quite often, the question arises as to the applicability of some "inconsistent" defences in our Criminal Code.[1] The principles and frontiers of these defences are fairly clear, both to the Bench and the Bar, but when such defences as self-defence, provocation and accident are raised simultaneously, the question of their exclusivity or mutuality becomes immanent. This paper attempts a synthesiszation of these defences under the Criminal Code and evaluates their mutual and/or exclusive applicability under our criminal justice system.

(a) The Defence of Self-Defence

Sections 286 and 287 of the Criminal Code make provisions for the defences of self-defence and distinguish between self-defence from provoked attack and self-defence from unprovoked attack. Under section 286, which provides for self-defence against unprovoked assault, the law is that -

> when a person is unlawfully assaulted, and has not provoked the assault, it is lawful for him to use such force to the assailant as is reasonably necessary to make effectual defence against the assault: Provided that the force used is not intended and is not such as is likely, to cause death or grievous harm.
>
> If the nature of the assault is such as to cause reasonable apprehension of death or grievous harm, and the person using force by way of defence

> believes, on reasonable grounds, that he cannot otherwise preserve the person defended from death or grievous harm, it is lawful for him to use any such force to the assailant as is necessary for defence, even though such force may cause death or grievous harm.

Section 286 contemplates two situations: (i) where the attack by the assailant is not intended to be fatal, but may cause *harm,* the accused relying on the first paragraph may use reasonable force to ward off the assault and such force must not be intended and must not be likely to cause death or grievous harm; and (ii) where the assailant makes a murderous attack on the accused, and believing that he cannot otherwise preserve his life, such accused is entitled to use any such force to the assailant in self-defence even though such force may cause death or grievous harm.[2]

The Criminal Code provides[3] that it is unlawful to kill any person unless such killing is authorised or justified or excused by law. It means therefore, that for an accused person to be guilty of murder under section 316 of the Code, the killing must be *unlawful,* meaning therefore that there could be circumstances under which a killing is lawful. Section 286 provides for such a circumstance because, the accused person, reasonably believing himself to be in immediate danger of death or grievous harm, kills the deceased who has offered such violent attack.[3a] The criminal law in such a situation says that the accused is not criminally responsible for such a killing (even if the killing was intentional)[4] and provides him with an absolute defence. Although it is not part of the requirements of our law under Section 286 of the Code, the common law required that the person attacked should retreat as far as possible before retaliating. We shall however discuss this requirement under section 287 of the Code.

Each time the defence of self-defence is raised particularly in homicidal offences, it is important to assess the nature and degree of the attack by the deceased, and determine whether such attack created in the mind of the accused, a reasonable apprehension of imminent death or grievous bodily harm.[5] The test of reasonableness is certainly objective because this defence is not ordinarily available to timid, nervous or easily excitable persons.[6] Apart from the test of reasonableness, the courts have always held that for the defence of self-defence to avail an accused person, regard must be had to all the circumstances of the case including the requirement that the retaliation must be commensurate in force with the gravity of the alleged attack.[7]

In *Alo Chukwu v. the State,8* the case for the prosecution was that on 6th August 1983, the day of the election for the President of Nigeria, the appellant was one of the Policemen posted to George-Ama to maintain law and order. The deceased was a Presiding Officer at George-Ama. At the end of the voting, the deceased together with others concerned with the officiating of the various voting stations, including the appellant and other policemen, went to the George-Ama waterside to join a boat to convey them and their voting materials to Okrika mainland. It was there they were thus awaiting the arrival of the boat that the appellant pointed his gun at the people waiting as described above. The deceased and some others who were waiting objected to the appellant pointing the gun at them. Shortly after, the appellant, at a very close range of about 3-4 yards, aimed the gun and pulled the trigger. The smoke (tear gas) grenade hit the deceased who fell down at the spot. The deceased was totally wounded and when he was carried to the hospital, he died. The defence of the appellant was that the villagers, at Waterside, where the team was to take a boat to Okrika, were shouting at them for not allowing them to rig the election and they then set on them and were beating him.

In holding that the defence of self-defence was unavailable to the appellant, the Supreme Court held, inter alia;

> assuming it was true the appellant was physically attacked by a mob, a claim disbelieved by the trial court, the act of self-defence must not only be against those that attacked him but must be commensurate in force with the gravity of the alleged attack. A patently dangerous weapon like a gun with a smoke shell cocked in it and fired directly at a person at close range could hardly be described as self-defence to an attack whose ferocity is unexplained by the appellant.

A case which could be regarded as the precursor to the above trenchant view of the Supreme Court was the decision of the Federal Supreme Court in *Bassey v. Queen*[8] where the court held that a plea of self-defence will not be upheld if the assault being defended is not such as to cause reasonable apprehension of death of grievous harm, and the force used is excessive in all circumstances. According to the court:

> the appellant received no injuries and was unable to show any on his person. In these circumstances we think that the assault on the appellant was not such as to cause reasonable apprehension of death or grievous harm and the force used by the appellant was excessive in all these circumstances.

Analagous to the requirement that the degree of retaliation must be commensurate in force with the gravity of the alleged attack, is the requirement that there should not be abysmal disparity in strength between the person offering the threat and the accused. This interpretation must be read into Section 286 because that Section provides that "... the person using force by way of defence believes, on reasonable grounds, that he cannot otherwise preserve the person defended from death or grievous harm..." In *Umana v. State,*[9] the Supreme Court held, inter alia.

> as respects the plea of self-defence, the learned trial Judge, quite rightly in our view, failed to see what the accused (aged 40) had to fear from the deceased (aged 60) who was not attacking him with any lethal or dangerous weapon so as to make the accused believe, on reasonable ground, that he could not otherwise save himself from death or grievous bodily harm...

To determine whether the present attack is sufficient to ground a defence under Section 286, the Court must also consider evidence of previous altercations or enmities and threats culminating in the present reasonable apprehension of death or grievous harm.[10] In *Beckford v. R*[11] the appellant, a police officer, while investigating a report that a man has been terrorising his family, shot and killed a man who ran out of the back of the house. At the trial of the accused for murder, the Judge directed the jury that he was entitled to be acquitted on the ground of self-defence if he had a reasonable belief that his life was in danger or that he was in danger of serious bodily harm. Although he was convicted on other grounds, the Privy Council quashed the conviction, holding that the accused was entitled to believe that he was in danger of imminent death as a result of previous terrorist acts by the deceased.

(b) Self Defence Against Provoked Assault

According to Section 287 of the Code

> when a person has unlawfully assaulted another or has provoked an assault from another, and that other assaults him with such violence as to cause reasonable apprehension of death or grievous harm, and to induce him to

believe, on reasonable grounds, that it is necessary for his preservation from death or grievous harm to use force in self-defence, he is not criminally responsible for using any such force as is reasonably necessary for such preservation, although such force may cause death or grievous harm.

The protection under Section 287 does not, however, extend to a case in which the person using force, which causes death or grievous harm, first began the assault with intent to kill or to do grievous harm to some person; nor to a case in which the person using force which causes death or grievous harm endeavoured to kill or to do grievous harm to some person; nor, in either case, unless, before such necessity arose, the person using such force declined further conflict, and quitted it or retreated from it as far as was practicable.[12]

The question of retreat is specifically provided for under section 287, but sometimes there is a confusion whether it is not also a requirement under Section 286. Of course, it is not part of our law of self-defence under Section 286 that the accused must have retreated as far as possible before killing his assailant. In *R v. McInness*,[13] the court held that retreat is only a material factor to be considered when judging reasonableness of conduct. Accordingly, Professor C.O. Okonkwo[14] has summarised the effect of Section 287 as follows:

(i) If D has unlawfully assaulted V or has provoked an assault from V and V assaults him in reasonable apprehension of death or grievous bodily harm, D may defend himself using such force as is reasonable for the purpose and may kill V if necessary.

(ii) But if D began the assault on V with intent to kill him or do him grievous bodily harm, or had tried to kill V before the need to defend himself arose, then it must be shown that D declined further conflict and retreated as far as practicable before the need to kill V arose.

Professor Okonkwo thinks that this is a very sensible provision because if D attacks V with intent to kill him or to do him grievous bodily harm, and V defends himself fiercely cutting D in danger of death, then if D succeeds in killing V, this is murder. He set out to kill V, succeeded in doing so, and his guilt is therefore clear. But if when V defended himself, D retreated, quitting the conflict, this terminates his initial *mens rea*. If his life is thereafter endangered, he may then kill in self-defence.[14a]

It may, sometimes, happen that two people are engaged in a ferocious or savage fight and in the process, one kills the other. The position of the law is that that killing is unlawful and is at least manslaughter (depending on the circumstances). However it may be difficult, in such a situation, to say whether the combatants are fighting or whether one is engaged in self-defence. If the former, the accused is guilting as aforesaid; but if the latter, the Supreme Court has decided in *Mgboko v. State*[15] that the defence of self-defence is available as a defence to a charge of murder which resulted from a fight if it is shown that the accused took reasonable steps to disengage or make some physical withdrawal. This view finds substantial support in the dictum of Lindley J. in an old case of *R v. Knock*[16] where he said:

> ...if a man attacks me, I am entitled to defend myself, and the difficulty arises in drawing the line between mere self defence and fighting. The test is this: a man defending himself does not want to fight, and defends himself solely to avoid fighting. Then, supposing a man attacks me and I defend myself, not intending or desiring to fight, but still fighting - in one sense - to defend myself, and I knock him down and thereby unintentionally kill him, that killing is accidental.

On the degree of withdrawal or disengagement from a fight to entitle the accused to rely on the defence of self defence, Lord Justice Widgery put it succinctly in *DPP v. Julien*[17] when he said:

> it is not, as we understand it, the law that a person threatened must take to his heels and run in the dramatic way suggested by Counsel; but what is necessary is that he should demonstrate by his actions that he does not want to fight. He must demonstrate that he is prepared to temporise and disengage and perhaps to make physical withdrawal; and that that is necessary as a feature of the justification of self-defence is true, in our opinion, whether the charge is a homicide charge or something less serious.

(c) Excessive Force/Defence

Section 298 of the Criminal Code provides that any person authorised by law to use force is criminally responsible for any excess, according to the nature and quality of the act which constitutes the excess. The criminal law permits the use of force in various circumstances such as in self-defence,[18] defence of dwelling house,[19] defence of property[20] or in defence of another.[21] In all these cases, the law expects that use of force should not exceed the maximum force allowed in such situations and which the law regards as reasonable. Anything beyond that is regarded as unreasonable and the defence collapses.

Section 298 of the Code does not say what happens in a situation, for instance, where an accused person has a right to self defence against unprovoked assault, but exceeds that degree of force which the law allows him. All that the section says is that he is liable for the excess of the force used. Because there is no specific provision in the code prescribing specific offence of using excessive force, this lacuna in the law (if we must call it one) creates the unfortunate situation where a defence of self-defence either succeeds as a whole and the accused is acquitted or the defence collapses as a result of excessive force used and the accused is convicted of murder.[21a] As stated earlier, the law has always recognised the right of a person to protect himself from attack and to act in the defence of others, etc and if necessary to inflict violence on another in so doing. If no more force is used than is reasonable to repel the attack such force is not unlawful and no crime is committed. In *R v. Chisam*[22] Lord Parker, CJ, approved the statement of the law in 10 *Halsbury's Law* (3rd ed.) p. 721 para 1382.

> where a forcible and violent felony is attempted upon the person of another, the party assaulted, or his servant, or any other person present, is entitled to repel by force, and if necessary, to kill the aggressor. There must be a reasonable necessity for the killing, or at least an honest belief based upon reasonable grounds that there is such a necessity...

Following this strong statement of the law, Lord Widgery, who succeeded Lord Parker as Lord Chief Justice, held in *R v. Fennell*[23] that

> where a person honestly and reasonably believes that he or his child is in imminent danger of injury, it would be unjust if he were deprived of the right to use reasonable force by way of defence merely because he had made some genuine mistake of fact.

The problem therefore arises as to what punishment is adequate in a charge of murder where an accused *ab initio* has a right to self defence but the only problem is that he has exceeded the degree of force which the law grants him. According to Mason, J, in *Viro v. R.*[24]

> ...the moral culpability of a person who kills another in defending himself but who fails in a plea of self-defence only because the force which he believed to be necessary exceeded that which was reasonably necessary falls short of the moral culpability ordinarily associated with murder.

As a result of serious death of Nigerian cases in this difficult area of our law,[25] two possible views can be canvassed:

(i) That the accused made a mistake as to his assessment of the gravity of the attack by his assailant thereby misjudging the degree of force to be employed by him to ward off the attack. In such a situation, "if the defender uses more force than is necessary for defence and kills the other party, the offence is manslaughter.[26]

(ii) That there is no criminal liability because the accused honestly and reasonably believes that he is in imminent danger of death or grievous harm and this honest and reasonable believe should entitle him to an absolute defence despite his mistake.

The present writer is in sympathy with the latter proposition because if there is an attack so that defence is reasonably necessary, it should be recognised that a person defending himself on the spur of the moment cannot weigh to a nicety the exact measure of his necessary or proportionate defensive action. Furthermore, a man about to be attacked does not have to wait for his assailant to strike the first lethal blow or fire the first shot; circumstances may warrant or justify a pre-emptive strike.[26a] In any event, the combined effect of Section 25 of the Criminal Code and the two sections on self-defence, i.e. Section 286 and 287, would be that if judged on the facts as he perceived them to exist, the accused will not be criminally responsible for the result of his act for Section 25 provides that a person who does or omits to do an act under an honest and reasonable but mistaken belief in the existence of any state of things *is not criminally responsible for the act or omission to any greater extent than if the real state of things had been such as he believed to exist*.[26b] This view finds support in the common law doctrine of necessity or what we usually refer to as extra-ordinary emergency (Section 26 of the Criminal Code) under our own law. At the heart of this defence is the perceived injustice of punishing violations of the law in circumstances in which the person had no other viable or reasonable choice available; the act was wrong but it is excused because it was realistically unavoidable.[26c]

if a jury thought that in a moment of unexpected anguish, a person attacked had only done what he honestly and instinctively thought was necessary that would be most potent evidence that only reasonable defensive action had been taken. A jury will be told that the defence of self-defence, where the evidence makes it raising possible, will only fail if the prosecution show beyond doubt that what the accused did was not by way of self-defence.[27]

(d) The Defence of Provocation

Section 318 of the Criminal Code provides that when a person unlawfully kills another in circumstances which, but for the provisions of the Section, would constitute murder, does the act which causes death;

i. in the heat of passion; ii. caused by sudden provocation; and iii. before there is time for his passion to cool; he is guilty of manslaughter only. Section 318 does not define provocation, but the Code in Section 283 attempts a definition of the term, provocation, by providing that:

> the term "provocation" used with reference to an offence of which an assault is an element, includes, except as hereinafter stated, any wrongful act or insult of such a nature as to be likely, when done to an ordinary person, or in the presence of an ordinary person to another person who is under his immediate care, or to whom he stands in a conjugal, parental, filial, or fraternal, relation, or in the relation of master or servant, to deprive him of the power of self-control and to induce him to assault the person by whom the act or insult is done or offered.
>
> When such an act or insult is done or offered by one person to another, or in presence of another to a person who is under the immediate care of that other, or to whom the latter stands in any such relation as aforesaid, the former is said to give to the latter provocation for an assault.
>
> A lawful act is not provocation to any person for an assault. An act which a person does in consequence of excitement given by another person in other to induce him to do the act, and thereby to furnish an excuse for committing an assault, is not provocation to that other person for an assault.
>
> An arrest which is unlawful is not necessarily provocation for an assault, but it may be evidence of provocation to a person who knows of the illegality.

From the above definition, it is clear that Section 283 defines provocation for purposes of Section 318 of the Code and the two sections must be read together.[28] Provocation in law, therefore, consists mainly of three elements:

(a) the act of provocation
(b) the loss of self-control, both actual and reasonable; or
(c) the retaliation being proportionate to the provocation.

To succeed on the defence of provocation, the three elements must co-exist. They are not detachable.[29] Although provocation, where successfully pleaded, provides an absolute defence for non-capital offences such as assault, it can never justify a killing; no matter how grave the provocation is. The Criminal Code regards any unlawful killing that does not come within Section 316 (which provides for the offence of murder) as manslaughter.[30]

Therefore, the most that a successful plea of provocation in a murder trial can do for an accused is to reduce the criminal liability of such a person to manslaughter.[31] This makes good legal sense because it is clear from the definition of provocation in Section 283 of the Criminal Code that a person who relies on it as a defence admits the commission of the assault or the doing of the intentional act, but seeks an excuse on the grounds of the wrongful act or insult done to him or some other person.

According to Lord Atkin in the leading case of *Andrews v. DPP*.[32]

> my Lords, of all crimes, manslaughter appears to afford most difficulties of definition, for it concerns homicide in so many and so varying conditions. From the early days, when any homicide involved penalty, the law has gradually evolved through successive differentiations and integrations until it recognises murder on the one hand, based mainly, though not exclusively, on an intention to kill, and manslaughter on the other hand, based mainly, though not exclusively on the absence of intention to kill, but the presence of an element of 'unlawfulness' which is the elusive factor.

Before the accused can rely on the defence of provocation, certain factors have to be taken into consideration.[33] For want of space, we shall not discuss these factors in detail, but would attempt to give necessary guide for further reading and research. From a proper construction of Section 283 of the Code, it is clear that the provocation offered by the deceased must be such as to cause a reasonable person to lose his self-control. The courts have held that the test is the effect which the act of provocation would have on a reasonable ordinary man, not the effect which it did actually have on the accused.[34] In *D.P.P v. Camplin*,[35] the House of Lords noted that a point of law of general public interest was whether on the prosecution for murder of a boy of 15, where the issue of provocation arises, the jury should be directed to consider the question whether the provocation was enough to make a reasonable man do as he did by reference to a "reasonable adult" or by reference to a "reasonable boy of 15." The House of Lords held that the boy's age was a relevant consideration in a plea of a defence of provocation. According to the court,

> that the boy was only 15 years of age at the time of the killing is the relevant characteristic of the accused in the instant case. It is a characteristic which may have its effect on temperament as well as physique... To require old heads on young shoulders is inconsistent with the law's compassion of human infirmity to which Sir Michael Foster ascribed the doctrine of provocation more than two centuries ago.

The second consideration for a successful plea of provocation is that the act must be done in the heat of passion caused by sudden provocation and before there is time for passion to cool.[36] In *Ajunwa v. State,*[37] the case for the prosecution was that in the course of an argument which occurred between the appellant, his wife and children on the one hand, and the deceased and his brothers on the other hand, a fight ensued and that during the fight the appellant went inside his house, brought out a double barrel gun and shot the deceased (his nephew) in the chest at every close range. The appellant did not deny the killing but claimed that he did so under great provocation as the deceased and his brothers were damaging his shop and were preparing to burn down his house. The Supreme Court held that there was no evidence of killing due to sudden provocation and in the heat of passion before there was time for passion to cool down because even if the appellant was provoked, there was sufficient time for him to cool down as he had time to run into his bedroom, collect his gun, advise his children to stay clear, before shooting the deceased twice.[38]

A corollary to the requirement that there must not be any cooling time between the time of the provocation and the act complained about is the requirement that the act must have been caused by sudden provocation i.e. a sudden wrongful act or insult.[39] The requirement of suddenness is not met by recounting previous wrongful acts and insults by the deceased, "but if the deceased subsequently does another wrongful act to the accused which may appear trifling, it is legitimate to take into account the previous provocative acts in order to determine whether the last wrongful act amounted to sufficient provocation."[40] This is especially so in cases of violent reaction by persons subjected to a long course of provocative conduct, including domestic violence, which may sap the resilience and resolve to retain self-control when the final confrontation erupts. However, it is our view that each case has to be considered against the blackcloth of its particular facts; the essence of the rule being to discourage retaliation and revenge. A direction to the jury that to find provocation, they had to find it in something done on the morning of the killing was approved in *R v. Brown,*[41] while a direction that they could review the whole of the deceased's conduct throughout the turbulent years preceding the death was characterised as "too generous" in *R v. Davies.*[42] Provocation by one person cannot justify the killing of another person who did not offer any provocation.[43] In *Ukwuenyi v. State*[44] the Supreme Court held that the trial judge was right in rejecting the defence of provocation raised by the 1st appellant on the ground that the provocation pleaded did not flow from the deceased but from the alleged conduct of another person.[45] However where there is a concerted attack by a group and actual provocation is offered by one of the aggressors, retaliation may be properly expended upon another in the group to found a defence of provocation; hence group retaliation must be the result of group provocation.[46]

Finally, resentment to the provocation must be proportionate to the act complained about. If the court finds or is satisfied that the accused committed the act as a result of provocation, the court must also consider the retaliation as against the type of provocation offered. In doing this the court must ask whether a reasonable man provoked in the way that the accused was provoked would retaliate in the way that the accused retaliated. If the court finds that a reasonable man would not retaliate in the way that the accused retaliated, the defence of provocation will fail because the mode of resentment does not bear a reasonable proportion to the provocation received.[47] In *Oladiran v. The State*[48] the Supreme Court held that the disproportion of the retaliation to the provocation is a factor for the court to consider in determining whether the accused had completely lost control of himself or was acting for a reason other than complete loss of self-control caused by sudden provocation.

Naturally, in every case where provocation is sought to be relied upon as a defence for murder, the killing must have involved an assault. This is an essential requirement since our thesis is that section 283 defines provocation, for the purposes of section 318, "with reference to an offence of which an assault is an element."[49]

(e) The Defence of Accident

Section 24 of the Criminal Code provides as follows:

> subject to the express provisions of the Code relating to negligent acts and omissions, a person is not criminally responsible for an act or omission, which occurs independently of the exercise of his will, or for an event which occurs b accident.
>
> Unless the intention to cause a particular result is expressly declared to be an element of the offence constituted, in whole or part, by an act or omission, the result intended to be caused by an act or omission is immaterial.
>
> Unless otherwise expressly declared, the motive by which a person is induced to do or omit to do an act, or to form an intention, is immaterial so far as regards criminal responsibility.

There is little doubt that the foregoing is the most far-reaching provision of the Criminal Code with respect to general defences. Its interpretation and application both by the Bar and the Bench have been somewhat problematic and streneous as shall be seen presently from a number of decided cases.[50] However, for easy and clear appreciation of the import of the provisions of Section 24 of the Code, it is always convenient to sub-divide the section into two limbs or parts. The first part or limb provides for "an act or omission which occurs independently of the exercise of his will" while the second limb or part provides for "an event which occurs by accident."

This division is particularly useful because the two limbs of Section 24 involve different parameters in their application.

As noted above, the first limb exculpates an accused person from criminal responsibility if the act or omission occurs independently of the exercise of his will; meaning that no criminal liability or responsibility attaches where the accused person did not *will* his act. Such situations may arise where the accused acts in a state of unconsciousness or hypnotism. It also excuses acts done while sleep waling. In *R v. Burgess*[51] Burgess and his friend and neighbour, Miss Curtis, spent an evening at her flat watching video tapes. She fell asleep. While she was asleep he hit her over the head with a bottle and the video recorder and then grasped her round the throat. When she cried out he appeared to come to his senses and showed great anxiety over what he has done. He was charged with wounding with intent. His defence was that he lacked the *mens rea* because he was sleepwalking which, he argued, was non-insane automatism. The court ruled that, assuming that he was not conscious at the time of the act, the medical evidence was evidence of insanity, and should be treated as such.

Judges are, however, reluctant, perhaps because of the consequences of a finding of insanity, to attach or label cases of automatism or sleepwalking as cases of insanity because if the accused was merely unconscious of what he was doing, then the most likely explanation was that he was in a hysterical dissociative state which should ordinarily exculpate him from criminal responsibility. Therefore, for an act to be willed it has to be proved that the act was a voluntary, conscious act by the accused, in full awareness of all the surrounding circumstances. In other words, the *actus reus* of an offence must include all the external elements of such an offence. An illiterate vendor who sells or otherwise disseminates seditious material should not be held criminally liable except he was *aware* that what he was selling was seditious material. It follows therefore that if the illiterate vendor was not *aware* of the seditious nature of the newspaper he was selling, and he was not negligent in finding out, then selling or otherwise disseminating seditious publication for which he stood charged occurred independently of the exercise of his will.[52]

> the expression "independently of" implies that D's will did not accompany what was done, that he was inadvertent to it. The effect of this on vicarious liability is obvious. The will that is in issue is D's will, not that of his servant. D will therefore not be criminally responsible for an act willed by his servant and not by himself.[53]

The second limb of Section 24 concerns the event of a man's act which means the result or consequences of such act. The limb provides that "a person is not criminally responsible for an event which occurs by accident." In other words, a man can "will" an act and the outcome, the result or the consequence of that "willed" act could be accidental.[54] *Stephen's Digest of the Criminal Law* defines an accidental event as:

> an event is said to be accidental when the act by which it is caused is not done with the intention of causing it, and when its occurrence as a consequence of such act is not so probable that a person of ordinary prudence ought, under the circumstances in which it is done, to take reasonable precautions against it.[55]

Therefore, an "accidental event is an event which was not intended by the actor, is not foreseen by him, and is not reasonably foreseeable. The test of foresight is objective. But if D foresees an event which no reasonable man would have foreseen, accident is ruled out."[56]

One difficulty which the application of Section 24 of the Code presents is with respect to the unlawful act doctrine. In other words, does the defence of accident apply to an event where the original act was manifestly unlawful.[57] It is our view that there is nothing in Section 24 of the Code which suggests that that section shall not avail an accused person merely because his act was unlawful. In *R v. Martyr*,[58] the court held that

> as to the construction of Section 23 of the Code (our Section 24) I adhere to the opinion expressed in *R v. Callaghan*[59] namely, that I am unable to see any suggestion in the Code that lawfulness or unlawfulness of an original act is a criterion of criminal responsibility for its accidental result.

There is a long line of judicial authorities[60] on the defence of accident, but the problem has always been on extricating the fine principles from the ghost of common law principle that an intentional *act* causing death even accidentally, must at least be manslaughter.[61] There is no basis for this because the defence of accident is a complete, absolute defence and the effect of a finding of accident is that the accused is not criminally responsible for the event.[62]

Are the Defences Considered Mutually Exclusive?

The three defences considered, namely, the defences of self-defence, provocation, and accident are no doubt, some of the most important defences in a charge of murder. From the wording of these defences it is sometimes thought that a plea of one precludes an accused person from founding a defence on the others, e.g. can self-defence and accident be pleaded simultaneously or in the alternative? Or can an accused anchor his defence on provocation and self-defence, on the same facts, considering that one is complete exculpation from criminal responsibility in a charge of murder while the other can at best reduce the offence to manslaughter?

In *Alo Chukwu v. The State,*[63] the defence relied on the defences of provocation, accident and self-defence simultaneously at the Supreme Court but the court held that "the defences of accident and those of provocation and self-defence are mutually exclusive." The Supreme Court further held that whole provocation and self-defence admit the intentional doing of the act that resulted in the injury, accident is a negation of intention. According to the court, whereas the defences can be considered separately where there is evidence in support, only the defences of provocation and self-defence may be raised on the same facts and it is not possible on the self-same facts also to rely on the defence of accident.[64] And in *Rasulu Oladipupo v. The State,*[65] which was a case of murder, the Supreme Court considered the propriety of raising the defences of provocation and accident at the same time on the same facts and held that the defences of provocation and accident founded on the same facts are inconsistent and irreconcilable for, whilst the defence of provocation is based on the admission of the facts as established, and merely raises a justification for the act, a defence of accident is predicated on the grounds that the event was not a result of the act intended by the accused, that he neither intended nor foresaw the result arising from his act.

There is no doubt that there are situations where it would be absurd or contradictory to plead the defences of self-defence and accident in the alternative, because in such a situation the accused would be saying "I deliberately and intentionally killed V; if I did not, V would have killed me."[65a] Therefore accident is ruled out. The same analogy may be drawn in the case of the defences of provocation and self-defence. I D's defence is that he was provoked and he ceased to be master of his mind and in that heat of passion, he did something unlawful i.e. a killing of another and the court finds that a reasonable man would have been provoked, he is not guilty of murder but of manslaughter. Therefore the issue of self-defence does not arise because D was not defending himself either under Section 286 or Section 287.

But there are also situations where it would be legitimate and reasonable to combine the defences of accident and self-defence or provocation and accident which the courts have not quite addressed. Perhaps, the difficulty in this area of our law is created by unfortunate principle in the early English law that a man is assumed to have intended the natural consequences of his act. This principle no doubt, may find good application and expression in the law of torts[66] but certainly it is not good law in crime because of the doctrine of accident and the protection thereunder provided by Section 24 of our Code. For example, it is a rule of the law of torts that if a man is injured by the defendant, it is no defence to the plaintiff's claim to damages that he would have suffered little or no damage or injury if he had not had an usually thin skull (the ego-shell skull) principle; or a particularly weak heart unknown to the defendant. In other words, once negligence is proved, the defendant takes the plaintiff as he finds him.[67]

The Supreme Court, with the utmost respect, went into this error in *Resulu Oladipupo's case*[68] a murder trial, where the court held that "although it is the law that a person should be taken to intend the natural and probable consequences of his action..." meaning that the old common law rule as decided in cases like *Nungu v. R*[69], creating a subjective approach to the ascertainment of intention, was still good law. But as was held in *Stapleton v. R*[70] the presumption that a man intends the natural consequences of his act is

> seldom helpful and always dangerous. For it either does no more than state a self-evident proposition of fact or it produces an illegitimate transfer of the burden of proof of a real issue of intent to the person denying the allegation.

The presumption of intention has been abolished in England by Section 8 of the Criminal Justice Act of 1967. Following that development the House of Lords in 1974 held in *Hyam v. D.P.P.*[71] that there is intention to cause death or grievous bodily harm if the accused deliberately and intentionally did an act knowing that death or grievous bodily harm was a probable consequence of it even though he did not desire it. Therefore, where an event was not intended, was not foreseeable and was not reasonably foreseeable, the accused should be allowed to take advantage of Section 24 of the Code. Such a situation presents itself where, for instance, D is engaged in a fight in self-defence.[72] If he inflicts a moderate blow that cannot ordinarily cause death or grievous harm on the operation site of his assailant (which fact is unknown to D) and he dies, there is no reason why D should not take advantage of the defences of self-defence and accident, considering that the death of the deceased was merely fortuitous. This, in our view will be a proper case for mutual application of the defences of self-defence and accident.

We dare say that by analogy, the same reasoning can apply to the defences of provocation and accident. If D is provoked into doing an act which was not intended to, and could not, cause death or grievous harm but death nevertheless occurs should D be denied the combined effect of the provisions of Sections 283 and 24 merely because it has been laid down that no amount of provocation can ever justify a killing?

In *Oladipupo v. The State,*[73] the appellant drove a commercial vehicle in which the deceased was a passenger. On getting to his destination, the deceased gave the appellant a N5 note and asked for his change. A fight soon broke out between the deceased and the appellant. They chased each other around the appellant's vehicle until the stage when the appellant brought out pliers from his vehicle and threw it at the deceased. The pliers hit the deceased on the head and he started bleeding, fell down and fainted. The cause of death was certified as "fracture of the skull." The appellant stated at the trial that he did not intend to harm or kill the deceased but that he threw the pliers at him to stop him from running away. The trial court rejected this story and sentenced him to death. The Court of Appeal confirmed the sentence. On further appeal to the Supreme Court, that court held, *inter alia:*

(i) Although it is the law that a person should be taken to intend the natural and probable consequences of his action, on the facts of this case as a whole, it cannot be inferred that the appellant either intended to kill or to cause grievous harm.

(ii) The defence of accident did not avail the appellant for, although, he may not have intended the death of the deceased by throwing a plier at him, the act of throwing the plier itself was not accidental.

(iii) The defences of provocation and accident founded on the same facts are inconsistent and irreconcilable.

After finding as a fact that the appellant did not intend to kill the deceased or cause him grievous harm, the Supreme Court accepted that the accused was provoked, but unfortunately mixed up, with respect, the application of the first and second limbs of Section 24. A proper application of the two limbs of Section 24 would have had the effect of recognising that the defence of provocation was available to the accused, and that the death of the deceased was accidental. The act of throwing the pliers was deliberate and intentional alright, but the result or consequence of that (event) was accidental. Our view on the mutuality of the defences of provocation and accident is supported by the reasoning of the Supreme Court in *Oladipupo's case* where the court held that "it is immaterial to the consideration of such defences whether they are contradictory or inconsistent, provided they are available on the totality of evidence before the court as in the case herein."[74] The effect of not combining the defences of provocation and accident is that an accused could be found not criminally responsible for murder or manslaughter of the deceased on a finding of accident, but criminally liable for assault. But if provocation was also pleaded it would then serve as a complete defence for the charge of assault.

Conclusion

It is our considered opinion that although the defences of provocation and self-defence may appear to be inconsistent and contradictory when applied alongside the defence of accident, the three defences are not mutually exclusive. Depending on the facts of each case, the courts should be able to find a defence of self-defence and accident, e.g. where there is a fight and the accused person is fighting in self-defence and accidentally hits a harmless blow on the operation site of the deceased, not knowing of his peculiarity. The same goes for the defences of provocation and accident as illustrated by *Oladipupo's case*.

Notes

1. Laws of the Federation of Nigeria (LFN) 1990 Cap. 77
2. *Laoye v. State (1985) NWLR (Pt.10) 832;* Nwogu v. State (1985) 3 NWLR (Pt.13) 467
3. section 306 C.C.

3a. *Ukaobasi Ajunwa v. State* (1988) 4 NWLR (Pt. 89) 380

4. *Laoye v. State* (1985) NWLR (Pt.10) 832. See also *Okpere v. State* (1971) 1 All NLR 1 where the Supreme Court held that "A man striking in self-defence may intend the dangerous, if not fatal consequences of his act. The circumstances under which he decided to do that which he did are extremely relevant in the consideration of his guilt or otherwise
5. Section 1 of the Criminal Code defines grievous harm as "any harm which amounts to a main or dangerous harm as defined in this Section (which means (harm endangering life)) or which seriously or permantly injures health, or which is likely so to injure health, or which extends to permanent disfigurement or to any permanent or serious injury to any external or internal organ, member, or sense.
6. *Akpan v. State,* (1992) 6 NWLR, 439. *R v. Onyeamaizu* (1958) NRNLR 93. The English Law now, however, appears to be abandoning the objective test for a subject test. Lord Lane CJ held in *R v. Williams* {1987} 3 All ER 411 at 415, and as correctly stating the law of self-defence in England, that:

   "The reasonableness or unreasonableness of the defendant's belief is material to the question of whether the belief was held by the defendant at all. If the belief was in infact held, its unreasonableness, so far as guilt or innocence is concerned, is neither here nor there. It is irrelevant...In a case of self-defence, where self-defence of the prevention of crime is concerned, if the jury come to the conclusion that the defendant believed, or may have believe, that he was being attacked...then the prosecution have not proved their case....Even if the jury come to the conclusion that the mistake was an unreasonable one, if the defendant may genuinely have been labouring under it, he is entitled to rely on it." The law Lord then concluded that the test to be applied for self-defence is that a person may use such force as is reasonable in the circumstances as he *honestly* believes them to be in the defence of himself or another. The fear however was that the abandonment of the objective standard demanded by the existence of reasonable grounds for belief will result in the success of too many spurious claims or self-defence, but both Professor Glanville Williams and Professor Smith appear to support this development believing that no jury will accept an accused's assertion that he believed he was about to be attacked without seriously considering the surrounding circumstances of each case. See Professor Glanville Williams, *Textbook of Criminal Law* (2nd ed., 1983)pp. 137-138 and Professor Smith, M. *Smith and Hogan, Criminal Law* (5th ed., 1983);;. 329-330). The test in Nigeria however is still the objective test.

7. *Alo Chukwu v. The State,* (1992) 1 NWLR (Pt. 217) p. 255 S.C.
8. *Ibid.*
9. (1963) 1 All NLR 280 at 283
9. (1972) 4 SC 164. See also *R v. Nwibo,* (1950) 19 N.L.R. 124; *The Queen v. Jinobu,* (1961) ALL NLR 627 Cf. *R v. Igwe* (1938) 4 WACA 117, where the deceased carrying a matchet pursued the accused. The accused disarmed him, felled him to the ground, and then killed the deceased with the deceased's own weapon. The Court held that the accused has a good defence under Section 286 because the accused reasonably believed that the deceased intended to kill him. According to the Court, the accused "may well have thought, and indeed not without reason, that he was engaged in a life and death fight with the deceased, if he could not kill the deceased he would certainly be killed by the accused."
10. *R v. Muratovic,* [1967] Qd. R. 15
11. [1987] 3 All Er 425, P.C.
12. Section 287, 2nd paragraph. *R v. Molnness* [1971] 3 All E.R. 295
13. *Op. cit*
14. Professor C.O. Okonkwo (SAN) (Unpublished monograph, on Homicide), Faculty of Law, University of Nigeria, Enugu Campus
15. Professor C.O. Okonkwo, *ibid*
16. (1972) 2 S.C. 123. See also *Nwaogu v. State,* (1992) 7 NWLR (Pt.254) 429 C.A.
16. (1877) 14 Cox 1 at 2. See, also, Okonkwo & Naish, *Criminal Law in Nigeria,* 2nd ed. (London: Sweet and Maxwell, 1980) p.224
17. (1969) 53 Cr. App. R. 407 at 411; (1969) 1 W.L.R. 839 at 843.
18. Sections 286 and 287 C.C.
19. S. 282 C.C.

20. Eg. Sections 289-293 C.C.
21. S.288 C.C.
22. *Chukwu v. State.* (1992) 1 NWLR (Pt.217) 255
22. (1963) 47 Cr. App. Rep. 130
23. [1971] 1 QB 428 at 431, [1970] 3 ALL ER 215 at 217
24. 919780 141 CLR 88 at 146-147
25. See, Professor C.O. Okonkwo, SAN, Excessive Self-Defence - Manslaughter in Nigeria" in Umezulike, I.A. and Nweze, C.C., (ed) *Perspectives in Law and Justice* - (Enugu: Fourth Dimension Publishing Co. Ltd, 1996) P. 296
26a. Smith and Hogan, *Criminal Law, Cases and Materials,* 5th ed. p. 311
26b. Emphasis mine
26c. See *Southwark London Borough Council v. Williams* [1971] Ch. 734; See also Dickson J. of the Supreme Court of Canada in *Perka v. Queen,* (1984) 13 DLR (4th) 1.
27. Per Taylor J. in *Queen v. Howe,* (1958) 100 C.L.R. 467
28. *Obaji v. State,* [1965] 1 ALL NLR 269
29. *Oladiran v. The State* (1986) 1 NWLR (Pt.14) 75 S.C.
30. *Udo v. Queen* (1964) 1 ALL NLR 21; *Onah v. State,* (1977) S.C. 69
31. See *Bassey v. Queen,* (1963) 1 All NLR 280; *Ajunwa v. The State,* (1988) 4 NWLR (Pt. 89) 380 S.C.
32. [1937] AC 576; [1937] 2 ALL ER 55, p.439. See also *R v. Stone and Dobinson* [1977] 2 ALL E.R. 341
33. See also *Chukwu v. The State* (1992) 1 NWLR (Pt.217) 255 S.C.
34. See Okonkwo & Naish, *Criminal Law in Nigeria,* ibid, *p.241.* See also *R v. Nwanjoku* (1937) 3 WACA 208; *R v. Adekanmi* (1944) 17 NLR 99
35. [1978] 2 ALL E.R. 168; [1978] 2 WLR 679
36. See Section 284 Criminal Code. See also *Obaji v. State* (1965) NMLR 417; *Ajunwa v. State, op. cit., Chukwu v. The State* (1992) 1 NWLR (Pt. 217) 255 S.C.
37. *Op. cit.*
38. Per Nnamani JSC, at p. 390. See also *R v. Green,* (1955) 15 WACA 73; *R v. Igwe,* 1963 FSC 83 where a plea of provocation was rejected on the ground that if there was any provocation, there was time for passion to cool because the accused had time to go to his home about a

mile away, brought a matchet and then killed the deceased. See also *Okpozo v. State,* [1966] NMLR 1

39. See *John v. Zaria N.A.* (1959) NRNLR 43; *Alonge v. R* (1964) 1 ALL NLR 115. See also *R v. Hayward* 172 ER 1188
40. Okonkwo & Naish, *op. cit.*, p.245
41. [1972] 2 ALL E.R. 1328; [1972] 2 QB 229
42. [1975] 1 ALL ER 890; [1975] QB 691
43. *R v. Ebok,* (1950 19 NLR 84; *Alo Chukwu v. The State,* (1992) 1 NWLR (Pt. 217) 255
44. (1989) 4 NWLR (Pt.114) 131 S.C.
45. See also *Omeninu v. State,* (1966) NMLR 356
46. *Ukwuenyi v. State, op. cit., Biruwa v. State* (1985) 3 NWLR (Pt. 11) 167; *Dumeni v. Queen* (1955) 15 WACA 75
47. F.n. *R.V. Nwanjoku,* (1937) 3 WACA 208 *Philips v. R* (1968) 53 Crim. App. Rep. 132, *Mancini v. DPP* (1942) AC 1; *R.V. Johnson* (1989) 89 Crim. APP. Rep. 148
48. F.n. (1986) 1 NWLR (Pt. 14) 75 S.C. See also *R.V. Akpankpan* (1956) 1 FSC
49. *Akpan v. State* [1970] 7 NWLR (Pt.160) p. 101
50. See generally, Professor C.O. Okonkwo SAN, *Nigerian Courts and Section 24 of the Criminal Code,* Law Monograph Series 1, (Onitsha: Meks Publishers (Nig.), N.D.)
51. [1991] 2 ALL E.R. 769
52. *Timbu Kolian v. The Queen* (1968) 119 CCR 47. See also section 51(c) Crim. Code
53. Professor C.O. Okonkwo, *op.cit* p.6. See also *Hunt v. Maloney,* (1959) Qd. R. 164
54. *Timbu Kolian v. Queen,* (1968) 119 C.L.R. 47
55. At p. 407
56. Professor C.O. Okonkwo, *op.cit., p.9. See also* R. v. Knutsen (1963) Qd. R. 157 at p. 166; *Vallance v. The Queen, (1961) 108 C.L.R. 56; Rasulu Oladipupo v. The State,* (1993) 6 NWLR, p. 131
57. *R v. Nameri,* (1951) 20 NLR 6, *Timbu Kolian v. The Queen, ibid, R v. Tralka,* (1965) Qd. R. 225, 232
58. (1962) Qd. R. 398
59. (1942) st. R. Qd. 40 at p. 50

60. See *Oladipupo v. The State,* (1993) 6 NWLR, 131; *Chukwu v. The State* (1992) 1 NWLR (Pt. 217) 255 S.C. *Ukut v. State* (1992) 5 NWLR (Pt.240) 240; *Daniels v. State,* (1991) 8 NWLR (Pt. 272) 715; *Audu Umoru v. The State* (1990) 2 NWLR (Pt. 138) 363; *Ijeoma v. State* (1990) 6 NWLR (Pt.158) 567; *Adelumola v. State* (1988) 1 NWLR (Pt.73) 683 S.C., *Ogbor v. State,* (1990) 3 NWLR (Pt. 139) 484, *Thomas v. The State,* (1994) 5 KLR 144 (SC), For a comprehensive and critical analysis of the defence of accident, See Professor C.O. Okonkwo SAN in *Nigerian Courts And Section 24 of the Criminal Code,* Law Monograph Series 1, *Op.cit* p. 9 *et seq.*

61. *Thomas v. The State* (1994) 5 KLR 144 S.C.

62. *Chukwu v. The State* (1992) 1 NWLR (Pt. 217) 255 S.C. See also the effect under the Penal Code in *Buba v. State,* (1992) 5 NWLR (Pt. 240) 202.

63. *Op.cit.* p.255

64. *Chukwu v. State, op.cit* at p. 270. See also *Akpan v. State* (1990) 7 NWLR (Pt.160) 101 at p. 111

65. [1993] 6 NWLR, 131

65a. See *R v. Igwe* (1938) 4 WACA 117

66. See *Re Polemis* (1921) 3 KB 560; *Thurgood v. Van den Burghs & Jurgens* (1951) 2 KB 537; *The Wagon Mound Overseas Tankship (UK) Ltd v. Morts Dock Engineering Co. Ltd,* (1961) A.C. 380; *Stewart v. West African Terminals Ltd* (1964) 2 Lloyd's Rep. 371; *Hughes v. Lord Advocate,* (1963) A.C. 837

67. *Smith v. Leech Brain & Co. Ltd* (1962) 2 Q.B. 405; *Robinson v. Post Office* (1974) 1 WLR 1175

68. [1993] 6 NWLR 13

69. (1953) 14 WACA 379; *R v. Amponsah* (1938) 4 WACA 120

70. (1952) 86 C.L.R. 358 at 365. See also *Smyth v. R* (1957) 98 CLR 163

71. [1975] A.C. 55; [1974] 2 ALL E.R. 41, [1974] 2 WLR 607

72. *R v. Knock, ibid.; Mgboko v. State,* (1972) 2 SC 123, *Oladipupo v. State* [1993] 6 NWLR 13

73. [1993]6 NWLR 131

74. F.n At P.140. See also *Stephen v. State* (1986) 5 NWLR (Pt.46) 978. For the position under the Penal Code, See *John Iwuaya Okonji v. The State,* (1987) 1 NWLR (Pt.52) 659 S.C.

CHAPTER 6

Teaching Students How To Write Legal Arguments

By
Dr Yvonne King
Senior Lecturer, Faculty.of Law,
Nnamdi Azikiwe University, Awka

Introduction

> Advocacy is the craft of persuasion. It is the means by which an attorney persuades a court to adopt his client's position as its own. The effective advocate will show a court that deciding in his favor would be logical and desirable, and that deciding for the other would not. Courts in an adversary system depend on advocates to illuminate the strengths and weaknesses of competing positions. The advocate thus assists courts in deciding cases. [1]

One of the challenges facing any lawyer writing an argument is illuminat[ing] the strengths and weaknesses of competing positions. The concept of identifying and distinguishing unfavorable authorities is at the core of effective advocacy and essential in writing appellate briefs. The Honorable P. Nnaemeka-Agu reminds us in his *Manual of Brief Writing* that "counsel is bound by the ethics of the profession to cite authorities known to him which are unfavorable to his case and try to explain away or distinguish them from the instant."[2]

In 1977,[3] brief writing was introduced in the Nigerian Supreme Court and in the country's Federal Court of Appeal in 1984.[4] However, since then, no provision within the LL.B. degree program or Nigerian Law School programs has been made to prepare for such a requirement at the Appeal Court and Supreme Court levels. In 1990, the author designed a Legal Writing class at the then Anambra State University of Science and Technology.[5] The objectives of the class evolved to include:

1. teaching students how to approach writing a legal argument;
2. instilling in students the value and necessity for accuracy and precision in their writing; and

3. assisting students with their writing generally.

Students of law often lack a framework for pursuing their theoretical coursework in the university. They dutifully attend their lectures, note the legal principles, read the assigned cases, which are sometimes not discussed, and complete their examinations. But, how do these theories function in the context of advocating for one's client? Moreover, how does one write a persuasive argument?

This article will focus on how to teach undergraduate law students skills that will assist them in preparing

> well-written briefs...[that] state the relevant facts and the law accurately and briefly and in a simple, lucid language, [and]...organised in such an orderly manner as to make them logical, intelligible, and easy to follow.[6]

Considerations For Writing A Brief

In writing appellate briefs, whether appellant's, respondent's, or appellant's reply, a lawyer must address three areas: 1) content, 2) organization, and 3) expression.

The content is primary because it constitutes the substance of the argument-the carefully and effectively stated issues, the favorable authorities, and the identification and distinguishing of the opponent's supportive cases and other legal authorities. The content must be accurate. Lawyers cannot manipulate the facts presented at trial nor those of cases they are relying upon in order to serve their clients' interests.

Organization is significant because it provides one with a framework for approaching the brief and facilitates the judges' reading, generally, and particularly their understanding of the lawyers' positions on the issues that are clearly delineated, and the authorities that are in support and in opposition.

And, finally, the expression reflected in the brief must be clear, precise, and grammatically correct. In addition to citing supportive authorities and distinguishing the opponent's, the language must be carefully selected to enhance the persuasiveness of the brief.

When there are no resources other than a lecturer and committed students, the challenge is developing an approach that will provide students with skills that will later assist them in writing appellate and respondent's briefs.

Pedagogical Approach

Anyone attempting to teach law students from Nigeria or other developing countries anything about writing, including developing legal arguments, will face numerous difficulties. The students' mother tongues are usually different from the language in which the law is practiced in their country. Also, in many instances, the size of the classes-usually more than 75 students-is too large to provide students timely and consistent feedback on their work, essential to helping them develop their writing generally and skills to write legal arguments particularly. Students need to write frequently, and, most importantly, be told what problems their writing exercises reveal before the next class. Such would be difficult for one lecturer with a class of more than 35 students, unless that person has no other subject to teach, which is rarely the case in any university.

This Legal Writing class has evolved from a compulsory segment of the Introduction to Advocacy course to a non-credit-elective, due to the increasing size of Law Faculty classes. Students sign-up for the course with the lecturer and are expected to attend weekly classes and interviews about their work. They do writing exercises in each class for one hour, and then attend an interview with the lecturer to discuss her written comments and students' questions or comments.

The writing exercise consists of responding to a question, which compels the student to take a position. Then the student must state one or more[7] reasons to support his/her position. The most challenging steps in the exercise are identifying and distinguishing one or more[8] opposing views. Students need to understand that as advocates in an adversarial legal system, they will always have opponents. Consequently, their opponents' arguments must be anticipated and distinguished. Demonstrating how the opponents' views do not apply must be embraced as an opportunity and not a step to be avoided.

In addition to practicing how to identify and distinguish opposing views, understanding the context for an advocate's need to look in both directions-for and against-is also important. When students realize that appellate judges when deciding appeals are confronted with competing positions and authorities based on briefs and, to a lesser extent, oral arguments, students can then begin to understand that ignoring or merely citing opposing authorities weakens their arguments because they have missed the opportunity to show how those authorities do not apply, which will help persuade the judges to rule in their client's favor.

The lecturer should pose questions to students that are based on topics they are familiar with, so they can easily complete the writing exercise. An example is, Do you believe that students found quilty of exam malpractice should be expelled? Students must be convinced that there is no right or wrong answer. What is critical is that their arguments must be consistent, persuasive, and accurate.

Students are usually given approximately 20 minutes to write their first drafts. It is interesting to note that most of the students do not know how to revise their work nor appreciate the importance of doing such. A second draft is foreign to many students. Probably they have never revised anything that they have ever written; therefore, we must help students realize by teaching them that writing is a process[9] and a form of critical thinking.[10] Professor Donald Murray, author of "one of the first popular books about teaching writing by a real writer"[11] informs us that

> [t]he writer understands that writing is a process, not a rigid procedure. He constantly rediscovers his subject...All effective writers know writing is rewriting. The inexperienced writer feels revision is a failure.[12]

During the writing exercise, students are compelled for 10 to 15 minutes to read their first drafts critically, make comments in the margins; cross out words, sentences or paragraphs; draw arrows to rearrange ideas, etc. Moreover, students are told, among other things, to look at their supportive reasons, whether they have successfully distinguished the opposing view, used correct grammar, be attentive to misspellings and choice of words.

Occasionally, students are directed to exchange their first drafts with their neighbors in order to benefit from their peers' critiques. It is important that students realize that assistance with their writing can be obtained from people other than lecturers, or, otherwise, those senior to them. Eventually, students will, ideally, recognize that critizing others' writing will help to improve their own. This will increase their awareness of certain writing problems, as well as expand their repertoire for solving some of them. Sharing their writing with their peers will also contribute to students developing a thick skin, which is a prerequisite for any writer, because one must learn to receive and appreciate constructive criticism. This is further reinforced by the interactions between students and the lecturer during the interviews.

Interviews

Students are provided the opportunity to individually discuss with the lecturer her comments on their weekly drafts written in class. The interviews provide students and the lecturer the privacy to be candid. However, often during the first couple of interviews, some students are defensive, which is understandable because probably most have never experienced having their work constructively or, otherwise, criticized. When the students begin to benefit from the interviews, they then realize the value of such critiques.

During the interviews, the lecturer frequently asks the students to read aloud some problem sentences to determine if they can recognize the errors. Although many students recognize their mistakes, they cannot describe nor correct them. Since English is their second, and in some cases third, language, they may not have intenalized the rules governing English usage, which at this stage is not essential. Students must realize that being able to recognize that a sentence does not sound correct can assist them in their writing. Then they face the challenge of building a repertoire of methods to solve their problems.

The amount of time for each interview varies based on the students' problems. For the past three years they have lasted between 5 and 30 minutes. In addition to discussing the students' writings, the interview provides the lecturer with an opportunity to get a sense of the students' commitment. This was particularly so when the course was compulsory. But, even now that Legal Writing is a non-credit course, students' consistent attendance at both weekly classes and interviews demonstrate their willingness to improve. Moreover, during the interview students pose questions, challenge the lecturer's assessment, and express their appreciation for the lecturers time.

Students' Problems

Students' problems in Legal Writing span the gamut due to the diverse levels of competency. Many make grammatical errors during the writing exercise, but recognize them immediately during the interview. However, there are students who are unable to identify these problems, even when they are highlighted with red ink. The lecturer then suggests various materials that these students can read on their own, in order to aid them in improving their use of English.

The focus of the Legal Writing class is to teach skills that will aid students in writing legal arguments at the appellate levels. Accuracy is essential in any appellate brief, consequently, the students are instructed not to make statements they cannot substantiate. For example, they are urged to avoid absolute terms, e.g., all and every. They are taught that baseless statements will weaken their arguments, considering that their opponents need only to indicate one instance that contradicts the all or every statement to defeat it. This is to heighten their awareness about the importance of accuracy.

Moreover, some students are unable to identify opposing views or the ones they do are not realistic. Often this is due to their not understanding the concept, particularly realizing it presents, not only a challenge but an opportunity to attack the opponent's argument. Repeated writing exercises in class and personal discussions in the interviews help students to grasp the concept of identifying and distinguishing opponents' views. This process, including students' reactions to the course, is documented by the lecturer to continue developing this relatively new area of study.

Students' Assessment

The student's registration number, arrival and departure times are documented, and the lecturer makes brief comments following each interview. The lecturer maintains a file for each student where his/her writing assignments are kept.

In order to obtain students' feedback on the usefulness of this class, at the end of the 1993/94 academic session the lecturer administered a questionnaire to the students she had taught the previous year. The purpose of the questionnaire was to learn from as many of the students as possible whether the course had assisted them in their next-year's studies. Considering that the interviews are an integral part of the pedagogical approach, the lecturer was anxious to know whether the interviews were helpful, if so, and in what ways.

Moreover, the questionnaire wanted to solicit how the students thought the course could be improved. All students were asked not to include their names or registration numbers, encouraging them to be as candid as possible. Out of 50 students 34 (68%) completed the questionnaire. A copy of the questionnaire can be found in Appendix 1 of the 34 respondents, 27 shard comments when solicited. The others merely answered "yes" or "no".

Majority (76%) of the students indicated that the Legal Writing course had assisted them in their final-year subjects and believed that it would help them in their legal practice.[34] However, 55% of the students believed that one hour was sufficient for the class, whereas, 45% thought that it should be increased to two hours. The interviews aided 82% of the respondents, primarily because it gave them an opportunity to see their mistakes and correct many of them instantly. A substantial majority (76%) thought that Legal Writing should be taught in other Nigerian Law Faculties.

Conclusion

Faculties of Law in Nigeria and elsewhere need to address the issue of teaching students how to write legal arguments. As lecturers, often with few resources, we must be more creative in providing students with viable skills that they can apply in legal practice. Initially, they must have a conceptual framework for writing arguments in an adversarial system. The essence of such a framework is recognizing the responsibility to cite opposing authorities and seizing the opportunity to distinguish them. Advocates are compelled to look in both directions-for and against.

We can no longer assume that university students know how to write just because they have reached this level in their formal educational careers. As trainers of lawyers, whose legal careers will include a great deal of writing, we have a responsibility to address this area, particularly those of us who are teaching students who will practice law in a language other than their mother tongues.

Our experiences need to be documented and shared amongst lecturers and attorneys, primarily because lecturers need the input of practicing attorneys and appellate judges. This lecturer, particularly, would appreciate any feedback to this initial effort in teaching law students skills that will contribute to their writing appellate briefs.

Notes

1. Hernbach and Singleton. *A Practical Guide to Legal Writing and Legal Method*, Rothman & Co.: Colorado, USA (1981)
2. *Manual of Brief Writing in the Court of Appeal and the Supreme Court of Nigeria*, 2nd ed., Fourth Dimension, Enugu: Nigeria, 1991, p. 16-17. *The Rules of Professional Conduct in the Legal Profession*, 4(a), also supports this position. "The conduct of the lawyer before the court...should be characterized by candour and fairness; and the lawyer should in court inform the presiding Judge of subsisting decided cases even where the decision is against the client. The lawyer is however entitled to distinguishing such case." as cited in Fawehinmi G. *Bench & Bar in Nigeria*, Nigerian Law Publications Ltd., Lagos, 1988, p.414
3. Cited by Honorable Justice Agu, P.N. *Manual of Brief Writing in the Court of Appeal and Supreme Court of Nigeria*, Fourth Dimension Publishing Co., Enugu, Nigeria. 1986, p.4
4. *Ibid*, p.5
5. In September 1992, this state institution became a federal institution, Nnamdi Azikiwe University. In 1993, all 50 students in the class eligible to take Legal Writing elected to do so even though it had become a non-credit course. Subsequent Legal Writing classes were limited to 35 to assist the students more effectively.
6. Nnaemeka-Agu, p. 5-6
7. Students are told how many supportive reasons to indicate due to time constraints.
8. *Ibid*
9. Tilly Warnock describes in *Writing is Critical Action* the writing process as four primary actions: "starting, sustaining, revising, and stopping." p.9
10. *Ibid*, p.11
11. Murray, D. A Writer Teaches Writing: *A Practical Method of Teaching Composition*, Boston: Houghten Mifflin, 1968, as cited in "*The Teaching of Writing in the United States*," L.Bouchard, Prospects, Vol. VIII, No.1, UNESCO, 1983, p.110

www.ingramcontent.com/pod-product-compliance
Ingram Content Group UK Ltd.
Pitfield, Milton Keynes, MK11 3LW, UK
UKHW040227290926
15471UKWH00001B/33